Y

D1538808

DATE DUE

GAYLORD			PRINTED IN U.S.A.

God vs. Darwin

The War between Evolution and Creationism in the Classroom

Mano Singham

ROWMAN & LITTLEFIELD EDUCATION
A division of
ROWMAN & LITTLEFIELD PUBLISHERS, INC.
Lanham • *New York* • *Toronto* • *Plymouth, UK*

Published by Rowman & Littlefield Education
A division of Rowman & Littlefield Publishers, Inc.
A wholly owned subsidiary of The Rowman & Littlefield Publishing
Group, Inc.
4501 Forbes Boulevard, Suite 200, Lanham, Maryland 20706
http://www.rowmaneducation.com

Estover Road, Plymouth PL6 7PY, United Kingdom

British Library Cataloguing in Publication Information Available

Library of Congress Cataloging-in-Publication Data

Singham, Mano.
   God vs. Darwin : the war between evolution and creationism in the
classroom / Mano Singham.
      p. cm.
   Includes bibliographical references and index.
   ISBN 978-1-60709-169-1 (cloth : alk. paper) — ISBN 978-1-60709-171-4
(electronic)
   1. Evolution (Biology)—Religious aspects—Christianity. 2. Human
evolution—Religious aspects—Christianity. 3. Scopes, John Thomas—
Trials, litigation, etc. 4. Evolution (Biology)—Study and teaching—Law
and legislation—Tennessee. 5. Evolution (Biology)—Study and teaching
(Secondary)—Pennsylvania—Dover (Township) 6. Creationism—
Study and teaching (Secondary)—Pennsylvania—Dover (Township)
7. Intelligent design (Teleology)—Study and teaching (Secondary)—
Pennsylvania—Dover (Township) I. Title.
   BT712.S56 2009
   231.7'6520973—dc22   2009013652

♾ ™ The paper used in this publication meets the minimum requirements
of American National Standard for Information Sciences—Permanence of
Paper for Printed Library Materials, ANSI/NISO Z39.48-1992.

Printed in the United States of America

This book is dedicated to
Frank and Loraine Tabakin

If everyone had friends like them,
we would all be happier and the
world would be a much better place.

Contents

Foreword

Perhaps no single issue has engendered as much ongoing legal controversy over a religious issue in education as the origins of the human race. Beginning with the so-called Scopes Monkey Trial in Dayton, Tennessee, in 1925—wherein a teacher successfully challenged a $100 fine for violating a state law that forbade the teaching of evolution in public school because it contradicted the literalist biblical interpretation of creation in Genesis[1]—and continuing to the present day, debate rages over what educators in public schools should teach students in science classes about human origins.

On the one hand are supporters of the mainstream point of view that students should be taught the generally accepted scientific theory of evolution. On the other hand are supporters of the literalist biblical perspective, sometimes referred to as "creation science," that students should be taught that the world was created in seven days according as presented in the book of Genesis. More recently, supporters of what may be considered an offshoot of the religious perspective, "intelligent design," have entered the fray.

Disagreements over the origins of humankind are so significant that litigation has reached the Supreme Court on the merits of the cases on two separate occasions In *Epperson v. Arkansas*,[2] the Court struck down a 1928 Arkansas law that forbade the teaching of evolution in state-supported schools since the statute required educators to disregard the theory of evolution because it conflicted with the literal biblical account of creation. Almost twenty years later, the Court invalidated a "balanced-treatment" law from Louisiana that forbade the teaching of "evolution science" in public elementary and secondary schools unless such lessons were accompanied by instruction on "creation science." In *Edwards v. Aguillard*,[3] the Court invalidated the law as unconstitutional because it lacked a secular purpose insofar as it was designed to present what was essentially a religious message.

Against a steady backdrop of cases on teaching about human origins, part of the torrent of litigation on wider issues under the Establishment Clause of the First Amendment to the U.S. Constitution, *God vs. Darwin: The War between Evolution and Creationism in the Classroom* presents a highly readable and comprehensive analysis of this fascinating area. With the perspective of a physicist rather than a lawyer, educator, or social scientist, Mano Singham applies his dispassionate scientific eye in such a way that he presents fresh insights into the ongoing controversy over who should control the content of curricula, scientific or otherwise, in public schools.

At its heart, *God vs. Darwin: The War between Evolution and Creationism in the Classroom* offers a valuable learning experience for all of those interested in education, religion, science, and the law. The book reveals a palpable tension regarding setting the parameters around the broader issue of control over school curricula. Put another way, as the Supreme Court reasoned in *Pierce v. Society of Sisters of the Holy Names of Jesus and Mary*, "the child is not the mere creature of the state; those who nurture him and direct his destiny have the right, coupled with the high duty, to recognize and prepare him for additional obligations."[4] Clearly, parental input is, and should be, important when dealing with the education of children. Yet, what is the role of professional educators when, even in according all due respect for the free exercise of religion by parents whose beliefs may differ from those of educators and others, they seek to promote an essentially religious vision concerning the origins of humankind, one that holds a minority position in Christianity as well as in the marketplace of ideas?

As part of the process of considering the past, present, and possible future of disagreements on teaching about the origins of humankind, Singham covers a vast amount of territory, including necessary reviews of the history of religion in American public schools generally and litigation under the Establishment Clause in particular. Following his review of the litigation on the evolution–creation science–intelligent design continuum, Singham seeks to balance such divergent perspectives as those held by biblical fundamentalists and what he describes at the "new atheists," both of whom are equally radical in their disdain for each other.

In sum, Singham's suggestion for seeking a way in which science and religion can learn to coexist peacefully in their own appropriate spheres is directly on point. As one who has earned graduate degrees in religion, law, and education, I find that Singham's apt conclusion—that science should rightfully operate in schools (and universities) with religion in homes (and, of course, churches or other houses of worship) rather than public schools—is a lesson that all should learn.

Charles J. Russo, MDiv, JD, EdD
Panzer Chair in Education and Adjunct Professor of Law
University of Dayton
Dayton, Ohio

NOTES

1. *Scopes v. State*, 289 S.W. 363 (Tenn. 1925).
2. *Epperson v. Arkansas*, 393 U.S. 97 (1968).
3. *Edwards v. Aguillard*, 482 U.S. 578 (1987).
4. *Pierce v. Society of Sisters of the Holy Names of Jesus and Mary*, 268 U.S. 510, 535 (1925).

Preface

It was with some trepidation that I undertook writing this book. Being neither a biologist nor a lawyer but instead a physicist, I knew I was undertaking a venture that was somewhat outside my area of expertise. I was helped by the fact that I was not a total stranger to the topic. Having a long-standing interest in the history and philosophy of science and having written in the past about the relationship between science and religion, I had explored many of the underlying issues at the heart of the attempts to undermine, or even discontinue, the teaching of evolution in U.S. public schools.

I was also forced to come to grips with this issue of evolution in the public school curriculum in 2001, in my capacity as a member of the advisory board that discussed and eventually set the science standards for K–12 education in the state of Ohio. This was at the height of the controversy about whether ideas based on intelligent design should be included in science standards and the associated curriculum.

In my work on that advisory board, I was astonished to discover that even the word "evolution" had not appeared in the previous standards due to its "controversial" nature. This stimulated my interest in investigating how it could possibly be that something so well established in the scientific community could be so toxic to large segments of the general population.

My involvement in these activities resulted in my being invited in 2002 to debate advocates of intelligent design in various forums, and my conversations with the attendees at these meetings gave me a broader understanding of why some religious groups fear evolution so much.

It is my hope that this book will be helpful to those who seek an understanding of the role that the teaching of evolution has played in adjudicating the broader question of the proper role of religion in the public sphere.

I thank James Paces and Barbara Forrest for carefully reading the manuscript in its early stages and making valuable suggestions and pointing out errors, and to Patti Belcher, Tom Koerner, and Elaine McGarraugh of Rowman & Littlefield for their enthusiastic support.

It is a pleasure to thank Dashi Singham and Ashali Singham who somehow seem to find the time, despite their own busy schedules and studies, to look over my book manuscripts and give me the kind of candid criticisms and suggestions for improvement that only daughters of an indulgent father can provide.

I owe a great debt to Jonathan Entin, professor of law and political science at Case Western Reserve University, who (despite his exceedingly busy schedule) took the time to go through an early version of the manuscript and offered a great many valuable suggestions, as well as educated me on the finer points of constitutional law and legal procedure. Needless to say, any errors that remain are entirely my fault.

Chapter 1

Introduction

One of the most intriguing legal struggles over the last century has involved the attempts by some people to counter what they see as the increasing secularization of public school education by trying to find ways to fit in some form of religion. While school prayer has been one important facet of these attempts and has perhaps received the most publicity, the teaching of evolution has also been, at least in the United States, the focus of many court cases involving various subtle shades of meaning and interpretation of the U.S. Constitution, testing in particular the limits of the Establishment Clause of the First Amendment, which states simply that "Congress shall make no law respecting an establishment of religion."

In this book, I will look at the history of the attempts over the last eighty years by those people who view evolution as antithetical to Christianity to undermine its teaching and at how the courts have responded to those efforts. That struggle can be divided into four main efforts.

The first attempt, resulting in the famous 1925 Scopes trial in Dayton, Tennessee, was to try to ban the teaching of evolution in public schools altogether. Although the Tennessee Supreme Court ruled that the law implementing the ban did not violate the state constitution, the *Scopes* verdict did not reach a federal appeals court or the U.S. Supreme Court; thus, its constitutionality under the First Amendment was never tested. But such laws banning the teaching of evolution were eventually ruled unconstitutional by the U.S. Supreme Court in 1968 in a different case that emerged from the state of Arkansas.

Next, came an attempt to balance the teaching of evolution and biblical stories of creation by requiring that both viewpoints receive "balanced treatment" in the classroom in terms of time and emphasis. This strategy had a rather shorter life, being ruled unconstitutional in 1975 by a U.S. court of appeals.

The third attempt took the form of another balanced-treatment requirement, except that now the teaching of evolution was to be accompanied by the teaching of something called "creation science," which consisted essentially of the same ideas behind the same biblical stories of creation as before, but now written in a quasisecular form stripped of all *overt* references to God, Christianity, the Bible, or religion. This strategy was ruled unconstitutional by the U.S. Supreme Court in 1987.

The final attempt entailed not explicitly requiring the teaching of alternative theories (something that the courts clearly frowned upon) but instead undermining the credibility of the theory of evolution by natural selection. This was done by arguing that students should be taught explicitly that evolution was "merely a theory" and not a well-established fact, that the evidence for it was weak, that there was a controversy within the scientific community about it, and that there exist phenomena that the theory cannot explain.

Furthermore, it was claimed, there existed a credible alternative theory called "intelligent design," which postulated that an unnamed and unidentified agency was necessary to explain key steps in biological development.

An essential component of this strategy of using intelligent design was to seek also to undermine the scientific principle of *methodological naturalism*, which ruled out invoking supernatural explanations (like intelligent design does) for physical phenomena. Methodological naturalism has long been an accepted working principle within the scientific community for a simple reason: as soon as one invoked a supernatural explanation for anything, research in that area simply stopped.

As paleontologist George Gaylord Simpson put it, "The progress of knowledge rigidly requires that no nonphysical postulate ever be admitted in connection with the study of physical phenomena. We do not know what is and what is not explicable in physical terms, and the researcher who is seeking explanations must seek physical explanations only."[1]

The pattern that emerges from these successive strategies is that the opposition to teaching evolution has gradually shifted and become diluted over time as the theory's evidentiary foundation has grown stronger scientifically and continues to strengthen. Direct attempts to oust evolution from public schools and insert religious ideas in its place have given way to the recognition that evolution is here to stay, that explicitly religious ideas will never replace it or make a reappearance in public schools, and that the best that can be hoped for is to chip away at the foundations of the theory.

As we trace this history, we will see that rather than the evolution cases themselves establishing important legal doctrines, cases turning on school prayer and other First Amendment religious issues unrelated to the teaching of evolution have resulted in the elaboration of the implications of the Establishment Clause. The interpretations arising out of, and precedents set by, these other cases have then influenced how the courts have adjudicated challenges to the teaching of evolution.

Because the legal questions surrounding the teaching of evolution in public schools are a fascinating subject in their own right, it is easy to forget that the important underlying question—who gets to determine what should be taught in public schools?—transcends legalities and raises fundamental, difficult, and as yet unresolved issues about the relationship of individuals to their government in a democratic society. Should it be the representatives to school boards and state and national legislatures elected by the communities funding the schools? Or should it be subject-matter experts in the disciplines being taught? Or should it be professional educators like teachers, principals, and professors in schools of education? Or should it be some combination of all these people?

On the one hand, one could argue a majoritarian point of view and say that local communities have the absolute right to determine what should be taught and that those who are disgruntled by their decisions can try to obtain redress through the ballot box.

Even if one takes this view, the issue of what constitutes the relevant decision-making community still remains problematic. Should it be the local community directly served by those schools and that pays for them through their taxes? Or should the larger groupings in which communities are embedded, such as state and national governments, also have a say? And how much autonomy should such bodies be permitted to have? Should they be allowed to mandate the teaching of ideas (such as that the Earth is six thousand years old or that humans originated in the Americas and not in Africa) that are flatly rejected by the community of scholars in that field of study? What if they want to teach a version of history that is rejected by professional historians but inculcates in their students a sense of racial or regional pride?

On the other hand, if one adopts a purely technocratic attitude that says that local communities should abdicate their right to determine what their children should be taught and delegate it to content experts or to professional educators, this carries with it the danger of creating an elitist technocracy that could, in the long run, undermine the democratic ideal.

Such awkward questions were less likely to arise in the distant past in the United States when the communities directly involved in public school education were local, smaller, and more homogeneous, thus less conscious of the need to accommodate minority viewpoints, and when the primary purpose of public (or "common") schools was seen primarily as religious education. Indeed, going back further to the early days of Western science, even the scientific communities believed in the divine revelation of nature as taught in the Bible and could not envisage any contradiction between the two. The role of scientists and other scholars was seen to be to explain how God had done what he had said he had done in the infallible religious texts.

But starting with Copernicus and Galileo, that narrow role for science became harder to sustain, and it was inevitable that scientists would, at least tacitly if not overtly, cut their ties with religion and start pursuing lines of inquiry that did not seek or require consistency with religious doctrines. The tremendous success of science following the Enlightenment validated this approach, and it then became the task of theologians to modify their beliefs about God to make them consistent with rapid advances in scientific knowledge; scientists no longer felt compelled to advance theories consistent with religion.

This shift caused a split within the religious community between those who adopted a "modernist" approach and those who adopted a "fundamentalist" approach to reconciling science with religion. Although both agreed that scientific and religious truths had to be consistent, they disagreed on what steps should be taken to achieve this end.

Modernists argued that in any apparent conflict between scientific truths and religious dogma, it is religious dogma that must undergo reinterpretation to re-achieve consistency.

Fundamentalists feared that such reinterpretations would destroy the credibility of the Bible by making it seem less than infallible. They wanted to draw lines in the sand beyond which they were not willing to compromise their beliefs. There are many such lines at play: the age of the Earth, the age of the universe, special creation of new species, a common ancestor for humans and apes, the nature of mind and matter, and so on. If science crossed those lines, the fundamentalists were unwilling to retreat as the modernist theologians tended to do but fought to force science to return behind the lines.

It was the theory of evolution that became, at least in the United States, a kind Maginot Line for many religious believers, the line that had to be defended at all costs. As a result, the high-profile science-religion legal battles have been fought in this arena, starting with the Scopes trial in Dayton, Tennessee, in 1925 and ending (at least as of this writing) with the intelligent design creationism (IDC) trial in Dover, Pennsylvania, in 2005.

In this book, I will examine the history of the legal battles over the teaching of evolution in public schools (which is itself embedded in the broader question of the role of religion in public schools and other agencies of the government) and discuss the decisions in various relevant cases, the creation of important constitutional precedents, the evolution of legal reasoning, the setting of the parameters of the decision-making process, and the influence of all these factors on the strategy of evolution's opponents.

It is good to bear in mind that all these issues revolve around that single fundamental question: who should get to decide what is taught in public schools?

NOTE

1. G. G. Simpson, *Tempo and Mode in Evolution* (New York: Columbia University Press, 1944), 76.

Chapter 2

The History behind
Inherit the Wind

It is almost impossible to think of the evolution-religion controversy (or the larger science-religion issue) in America without immediately calling to mind the famous Scopes Monkey Trial of 1925, in which a high school teacher, John T. Scopes, was prosecuted for teaching evolution in the state of Tennessee. That event has become a touchstone, framing the issue in a way that is hard to shake.

In some ways, this is odd because that case played only a very minor role legally, setting no important precedent. It did not actually resolve anything and did not even deal with the weighty constitutional issues that now surround the issue of teaching evolution in public school classrooms.

As an example, two recent books[1] aimed at legal scholars and dealing solely with the relationship between church and state never even mention the Scopes case. Yet, because of a curious confluence of factors, the shadow of the Scopes trial has hovered over all subsequent public and legal discussions of the teaching of evolution in schools in a way that is completely disproportional to the case's actual legal significance.

As is often true of great myths, when examined closely, the actual events behind them are less sharply drawn than the legend, but fascinating nonetheless. From the beginning, the Scopes trial captured the popular imagination as distilling the essence of the conflict between science and religion, on a par with the trial of Galileo for his support of Copernican views. But just as the myths about the Copernican revolution have supplanted the more interesting actual history,[2] so have the myths about the Scopes trial obscured the fascinating real account.

The Scopes "trial of the century" became the stuff of legend and shrouded in myth from the very beginning. How could it not when the subject matter of the case aroused strong passions nationwide, when the two main protagonists, William Jennings Bryan (for the prosecution) and Clarence Darrow (for the defense), were flamboyant, colorful, high-profile characters, and when the national and world media and commentators (especially the acerbic journalist H. L. Mencken) covered the trial? Right from the start, the spectacle overshadowed the facts.

After 1955, public perceptions of the trial's significance grew even more inflated, and its implications became even more distorted, with the long-running Broadway play *Inherit the Wind*, later made into a hugely successful 1960 film starring Spencer Tracy and Frederic March. The play's authors, Jerome Lawrence and Robert E. Lee, were not really seeking to dramatize the trial itself. They fictionalized the events of the Scopes trial in order to make it into a vehicle to warn of the dangers of McCarthyist blacklisting, which was going on in their own time, and used the trial's religion-science conflict as a proxy for the contemporary fight to retain freedom of speech and freedom of association.

The writers did not claim that their play was an accurate history of the trial and even tried to distance themselves from that charge by changing the names, places, and dates of the associated people and events, even adding new characters and plot devices, such as a love interest for Scopes. But the disguises they used were too thin. Despite their intention to use the Scopes trial for purely allegorical purposes, their portrayal resembled reality too closely and has become the foundation of the folklore surrounding the Scopes trial, forever creating confusion in the minds of people as to what really happened.

Largely because of the play and film, the trial is now recalled as an epic clash between the forces of narrow religious dogma and obscurantism (represented by orator and three-time Democratic presidential candidate William Jennings Bryan) and the forces of science, progress, enlightenment, and secularism (represented by famed trial attorney Clarence Darrow).

In a vivid scene toward the end of the film, which has left the most lasting impression, Henry Drummond (the name given to the

Darrow-like character) puts Matthew Harrison Brady (representing William Jennings Bryan) on the witness stand and, with a withering series of questions focusing on the age of the Earth, the story of Jonah and the whale, and the like, shows the foolishness of holding on to literal biblical beliefs in the face of science, reducing Brady to a mass of babbling and blubbering incoherence and making him a laughing stock in the courtroom and nationwide. Brady soon after collapses and dies on the courtroom floor.

While the real trial did end with Darrow putting Bryan on the stand and the cross-examination did bring out the difficulties with taking the Bible literally, what happened during the questioning was more complex, and Bryan died peacefully in his sleep five days after the trial.

In order to get behind the myths and see why the Scopes trial has become so emblematic of the science-religion conflict in America, we first have to understand the historical context in which it occurred.

Note that the theory of evolution by natural selection was first publicly proposed in 1858.[3] The basic idea of the evolution of species predated Charles Darwin himself, but the publication in November of the following year of Darwin's groundbreaking book *On the Origin of Species*,[4] with its comprehensive marshalling of the facts and arguments supporting the theory, resulted in almost the entire

Charles Darwin (1809–1882) was the son, grandson, and brother of somewhat freethinking Unitarians. His grandfather Erasmus Darwin had himself published a book, *Zoonomia*, containing evolutionary ideas. Although Charles Darwin started out as religious in a fairly orthodox way and believed in the theory of special creation of all species, his fieldwork on the *Beagle* and subsequent studies led him away from religion so that by the age of forty he had become an agnostic. His transition to disbelief was hastened by the death of his beloved daughter, Annie, from a mysterious wasting illness at the tender age of ten.

Darwin married his cousin Emma, who was devoutly religious, and his disbelief was a source of tension between an otherwise devoted and loving couple.

scientific establishment's coalescing around the basic assumption that evolution had indeed occurred. By the end of the nineteenth century, the idea that all species were descended with modification from common ancestors was widely accepted and had been taught in schools for some time.

So why, in 1925, did the sleepy little town of Dayton, Tennessee, become the focal point for this "trial of the century"? What made evolution belatedly so toxic? To understand why it took about sixty years for the full flowering of anti-Darwinian sentiment to appear in the United States, we need to understand a little more about Darwin's theory and that it involved several features.

Really disturbing about Darwin's theory was not so much the idea of evolution itself (although that was problematic enough for more fundamentalist religious believers) but his theory of natural selection as the *mechanism* for the process of evolution. Properly understood, this ruled out any *direction* for evolution.

According to natural selection, how organisms evolve depends on a combination of chance mutations and the environments in which organisms find themselves. While the environments strongly influence which organisms survive to pass on their characteristics to their progeny, there is no larger purpose behind the process. Hence, if natural selection were accepted as a mechanism, there would be no reason to think that human beings were *destined* to appear, thus destroying the idea that our species is somehow special or that there is any externally imposed purpose to life.

This important element of Darwin's theory was particularly upsetting to religious believers and was not easily accepted even by the scientific community of his time. Many scientists (in addition to laypeople) did not accept this lack of direction or purpose and proposed alternative mechanisms for evolution that retained them. As a result, the idea of natural selection as the fundamental mechanism for the evolutionary process went into a period of decline, even as the fact of evolution was accepted.[5]

Some of these alternative theories were modified forms of *Lamarckism*, the idea that characteristics acquired by an organism during its lifetime that enabled it to survive better were somehow transmitted to the entities in the body that carried inherited traits to the organism's progeny.

Another alternative was the theory of *orthogenesis*, which suggested that evolution followed a path determined by forces originating within the organisms themselves. This meant that it was possible to think that the laws of evolution contained within them forces that guaranteed the eventual emergence of the human species.

Such theories had the reassuring feature that there was some sort of deliberate and directed progression in evolution, enabling their believers to continue thinking of human beings as special and as the preordained end point of the process. The idea that human beings were special in the eyes of God could thus be retained, giving religious believers the comfort that their lives had the external meaning that they sought. The theory of evolution by natural selection offered no such assurances.

By the end of the nineteenth century, the theory of natural selection (though not evolution as a whole) seemed to be in full retreat. But the year 1900 saw the rediscovery of Gregor Mendel's 1865 work on genetics. Initially, this new knowledge seemed to work against Darwinian natural selection, further hastening its demise.

But beginning around 1910, the new field of population genetics was born, coupling Darwinian natural selection with Mendelian genetics and creating what is now called the neo-Darwinian synthesis. The mathematical analyses of scientists such as J. B. S. Haldane, Sewall Wright, and R. A. Fisher led to the resurgence of the idea of natural selection as the prime mechanism for evolution.[6] By around 1920, the reversal was complete. Darwin's theory of natural selection was ascendant and has remained so ever since, growing even stronger with time.

As a consequence of this dominance, however, the idea that human beings were somehow designed by God and had a special purpose was no longer seen as credible and indeed came to be perceived as incompatible with science. This was quite plausibly a significant reason for the seemingly belated rise of religious opposition to the theory of evolution that culminated in the Tennessee legislation.

NOTES

1. Marci A. Hamilton, *God v. the Gavel: Religion and the Rule of Law* (New York: Cambridge University Press, 2005), and Philip Hamburger, *Separation of Church and State* (Cambridge, MA: Harvard University Press, 2002).

2. Mano Singham, "The Copernican Myths," *Physics Today* (December 2007): 48.

3. The papers by Charles Darwin and Alfred Russell Wallace giving the outlines of this theory were presented on July 1, 1858, at a meeting of the Linnean Society in London.

4. Charles Darwin, *On the Origin of Species* (London: John Murray, 1859).

5. Peter J. Bowler, *The Eclipse of Darwinism* (Baltimore: Johns Hopkins University Press, 1983).

6. William B. Provine, *The Origins of Theoretical Population Genetics* (Chicago: University of Chicago Press, 2001).

Chapter 3

The Rising Religious Opposition to Evolution

Because of a mixture of chance and design, Dayton just happened to be the place where there occurred a collision between two trains of events, one emerging from the rising unease with the implications of Darwinian thinking for Christian beliefs and the other from concerns about infringements on the fundamental rights of free speech and free association following the post–World War I emergence of the Soviet Union and the subsequent "Red Scare."

The religious train arose due to unease over what the theory of evolution by natural selection implied for religious beliefs. This unease had been simmering for some time and became more accentuated as the full implications of Darwin's theory became better understood.

There were varying degrees of religious opposition to the theory of evolution. Some felt that allowing for any evolution at all for any species contradicted the biblical account of all species being specially created by God. Others were willing to tolerate the idea of all species *other than humans* being evolutionarily linked but found the idea that human beings were also part of the great tree of evolutionary descent repugnant as it implied that we were no different from other mammals, thus neither made in the image of God nor possessed of an immortal soul. Yet others were willing to include humans in that genealogy as long as there was a special caveat allowing for the insertion of the human soul that was not part of the theory. And yet others were willing to forego even that as long as there was some *directionality* to evolution, some guiding purpose to it that could give their lives some meaning.

Williams Jennings Bryan, champion of the antievolution cause, belonged to the second group, which sought to exclude just humans from the evolutionary process. A devoutly religious Christian and also a political populist, he supported many progressive causes while championing the underdog and fighting for the rights of the poor against their exploiters. Because of this, he acquired the nickname "the Great Commoner," as well as the moniker "the Boy Orator," which he earned early in life because of the skill he displayed as a public speaker.

He supported a basically majoritarian democratic view, holding that people, through their collective voice, had the final say in how they were to be governed. As such, he opposed elitist ideas, and he saw evolutionary theory as a doctrine that was being imposed on people, against their will, by a scientific elite.

It is a mistake to think that Bryan's opposition to the teaching of evolution was motivated only by religion. In fact, although he did oppose Darwinian thinking because of his religious beliefs and his fears that the theory left no room for God, he also opposed the claims of the so-called social Darwinists of that time, people like Herbert Spencer, who tried to extend Darwinian natural selection to explain the structures of human society and argued that "survival of the fittest" meant that harsh social conditions were inevitable and maybe even desirable since they would weed out those who were "unfit," thus improving humanity in the long run.

The robber barons of the era, people like Andrew Carnegie and John D. Rockefeller, who had made enormous fortunes amid widespread poverty, also took comfort from social Darwinism since it seemed to bestow a seal of approval on them and their actions, suggesting that their success was due to their exceptional "fitness" for the world of business and their innate gifts rather than their ruthless and exploitative business practices.

Bryan saw Darwin's ideas as the root of this particular evil, saying, "The Darwinian theory represents man as reaching his present perfection by the operation of the law of hate—the merciless law by which the strong crowd out the weak."[1]

Another factor at play in popular opposition to Darwinism was the rise of eugenics and its suggestion that the human race, just like livestock, could be improved by selective breeding, such as by segregating those people who were seen as "defective" and preventing them from having children. Many viewed eugenics as an abominable and inhumane practice, and those opposed to evolution saw it as a direct consequence of Darwinian thinking applied to humans—and dangerously close to playing God.

Their linking of Darwinian evolutionary theory with eugenics was buttressed by the fact that one of the founders of this new field (and the person who coined the name) was the British polymath Francis Galton, who happened to be Darwin's cousin and one of the earliest supporters of Darwin's theory.

Bryan was a humane and peace-loving man who even resigned in 1915 from his position as secretary of state in the administration of President Woodrow Wilson when it looked like Wilson was taking the country into World War I. That war gave Bryan yet another reason to oppose Darwinism as he was strongly influenced by some books written at that time arguing that the war was due to Darwinian principles at work among nations.[2]

Bryan opposed the excesses of both capitalism and militarism and also rejected any kind of social engineering at the expense of the poor. He saw Darwinism as a major source of all those evils and thus as a pernicious idea that had to be defeated. Removing its teaching from public schools was seen as an essential step in its ultimate eradication.

In order to appreciate Bryan's testimony in the Scopes trial, it is necessary to understand something of his religious views in the context of his times. In those days, as now, religious believers were split between those who took the Bible as an inerrant literal record of historical events and those who allowed for some level of interpretive license, whereby some events could be interpreted metaphorically so as not to clash with scientific truths.

A fairly sophisticated religious believer, well-read and knowledgeable about many subjects, including science, Bryan was unfairly portrayed as a pompous, buffoonish, dogmatic fundamentalist in the play and film *Inherit the Wind*. Although he would have considered himself a religious fundamentalist, Bryan was not as extreme a fundamentalist as today's creationists and did not interpret the Bible quite as literally.

Bryan belonged to the "gap" or "ruin and reconstruction" school of Christian thought. Such people were not committed to a six-thousand-year-old Earth; they believed that the days of creation described in the book of Genesis were metaphorical and represented "ages" that could stand for enough years to be consistent with the geological evidence.[3] This approach "allows for a very old, unspecified age of the universe, in which matter was first created, followed by non-human life and the formation of fossils. This creation process could have involved multiple cataclysms and creations and is flexible enough to accommodate most geologic evidence."[4]

Bryan was also willing to go along with a *limited* form of evolution as long as it kept humans out of the tree of evolved life and made them special creations. But he would not go as far as the modernist theologians of his time, who adopted "theistic evolution," which accepted the idea that humans and apes had common ancestors and saw God's role as somehow *guiding* the process of evolution, making it an early form of what is now called "intelligent design" creationism. Bryan did believe in the biblical stories of the creation of Adam and Eve in the Garden of Eden and the great flood of Noah.

In a 1922 newspaper essay,[5] Bryan explained clearly what he believed and the sources of his objections to the teaching of evolution in public schools.

> The only part of evolution in which any considerable interest is felt is evolution applied to man. A hypothesis in regard to the rocks and plant life does not affect the philosophy upon which life is built. Evolution applied to fish, birds and beasts would not materially affect man's view of his own responsibilities, except as the acceptance of an unsupported hypothesis as to these would be used to support a similar hypothesis as applied to man. . . .
>
> Christianity has nothing to fear from any *truth*; no *fact* disturbs the Christian religion or the Christian. It is the unsupported *guess* that is substituted for science to which opposition is made, and I think the objection is a valid one. (Italics in original)

He added that the falsehood of some idea like evolution did not, by itself, warrant opposition unless it was also harmful. He then placed his finger on why he thought evolution was damaging and, in the process, summarized accurately the consequences of taking the theory of evolution seriously, showing a much better understanding of the theory's implications than even many of today's religious supporters of evolutionary theory.

> It entirely changes one's view of life and undermines faith in the Bible. Evolution has no place for the supernatural. . . .
>
> Evolution proposes to bring all the processes of nature within the comprehension of man by making it the explanation of everything that is known. . . .

Evolution attempts to solve the mystery of life by suggesting a process of development commencing "in the dawn of time" and continuing uninterrupted until now. . . .

If a man accepts Darwinism, or evolution applied to man, and is consistent, he rejects the miracle and the supernatural as impossible. . . .

If he is consistent, he will go through the Old Testament step by step and cut out all the miracles and all the supernatural. He will then take up the New Testament and cut out all the supernatural—the virgin birth of Christ, His miracles and His resurrection, leaving the Bible a story book without binding authority upon the conscience of man.

Although Bryan's motives in drawing the consequences of evolutionary thinking in such dire terms for Christians may have been to scare them into backing his movement against the teaching of evolution, he is exactly right in his analysis. If one is consistent in applying the theory of evolution by natural selection, one has little choice but to reject God's intervention anywhere in the process.

Philosopher and cognitive scientist Daniel C. Dennett[6] speaks of the theory of natural selection as being like a mythical "universal acid," so potent and corrosive that once created it cannot be contained or restricted in any way but breaks through all barriers until it reaches into every space. Once you accept the theory of evolution by natural selection as applying in *any* area of life, there is no way to prevent it being used to explain *every* aspect of life.

To add force to his argument that teaching the theory of evolution was dangerous for Christian beliefs because it would cause people, especially young people at the age when they are challenging authority, to doubt the existence of God, Bryan pointed out how Darwin himself had started out in life as a religious person and became an agnostic as a result of his work: "If Darwinism could make an agnostic of Darwin, what is its effect likely to be upon students to whom Darwinism is taught at the very age when they are throwing off parental authority and becoming independent? Darwin's guess gives the student an excuse for rejecting the authority of God, an excuse that appeals to him more strongly at this age than at any other age in life."

In that same essay, he dismissed theistic evolutionists and their idea that God only created the laws of evolution and then did nothing else. He said that they put "God so far away that He ceases to be a present influence in the life. . . . Why should we want to imprison God in an impenetrable past? . . . Why not allow Him to work now?"

Thus, Bryan saw acceptance of human evolution in any form, the-istic or otherwise, as a very slippery slope that led to no good end: "Evolution naturally leads to agnosticism and, if continued, finally to atheism."

But while he disliked evolution on religious grounds and because he felt that it led to abhorrent social policies, those were not his only reasons for opposing its being taught in schools. He said he also ob-jected because he felt that the theory had not been shown to be true. And if it were not true, then those who taught it were merely teach-ing a doctrine, not scientific truth, and he saw no reason why they should have the right to teach in public schools what he considered an atheistic doctrine if religious doctrines were not allowed.

The crux of his objections to the teaching of evolution was as fol-lows:

> The real question is, Did God use evolution as His plan? If it could be shown that man, instead of being made in the image of God, is a de-velopment of beasts we would have to accept it, regardless of its effect, for truth is truth and must prevail. . . .
>
> Those who teach Darwinism are undermining the faith of Chris-tians. . . . Christians do not object to freedom of speech. . . . Christians do not dispute the right of any teacher to be agnostic or atheistic, but Christians do deny the right of agnostics and atheists to use the public schools as a forum for the teaching of their doctrines.
>
> The Bible has in many places been excluded from the schools on the ground that religion should not be taught by those paid by public taxa-tion. If this doctrine is sound, what right have the enemies of religion to teach irreligion in the public schools? If the Bible cannot be taught, why should Christian taxpayers permit the teaching of guesses that make the Bible a lie?

Bryan was making some very interesting points. In those early re-ligious arguments against evolution, one finds many themes that are echoed today: that the theory of evolution is only a hypothesis, a theory and not a fact, that it lacks supporting evidence, that an increasing number of scientists disbelieve it, and that it contradicts the Bible.

This was how one side in the conflict approached the Scopes trial, arguing that teaching evolution in schools while not teaching bibli-cal theories gave one doctrine an unfair advantage over the other. It is an argument that has persisted down to this day.

NOTES

1. Edward J. Larson, *Summer for the Gods* (Cambridge, MA: Harvard University Press, 1997), 39.

2. Larson, *Summer for the Gods*, 40.

3. For a fascinating account of the history of creationism and that movement's evolving views, see the book by Ronald Numbers, *The Creationists* (New York: Random House, 1992).

4. Mano Singham, *Quest for Truth: Scientific Progress and Religious Beliefs* (Bloomington, IN: Phi Delta Kappan Educational Foundation, 2000), 9.

5. William Jennings Bryan, "God and Evolution," *New York Times*, February 26, 1922, 84.

6. Daniel C. Dennett, *Darwin's Dangerous Idea* (New York: Simon & Schuster, 1995).

Chapter 4

The Free Speech Train

As William Jennings Bryan warned of the dangers of teaching what he called the "doctrine" of evolution in public schools while at the same time excluding religious doctrine, the other train of events that led to the collision in Dayton in the Scopes trial was the publicly expressed concern by the newly formed American Civil Liberties Union (ACLU) regarding what it felt were infringements on academic freedom, with teachers being fired for advocating unpopular views.

Following the worldwide rise of Communist ideas that ultimately led to the Russian Revolution in 1917, the "Red Scare" came into force in the United States, and state legislatures were proposing laws that harassed and called for the dismissal and even arrest of anyone who spoke in favor of "socialism, communism, anarchism, bolshevism, pacifism, [or] the international labor movement."[1]

In 1915, the also newly formed American Association of University Professors (AAUP) had presented its General Declaration of Principles, which addressed the issue of academic freedom. It said that those colleges specifically created to promote certain doctrines (for example, private colleges established by religious denominations) need not adhere to academic freedom and thus were free to have on their faculty only those who subscribed to their doctrines. But those institutions that received public funds "have no moral right to bind the reason or conscience of any professor."[2]

In 1924, the ACLU issued a statement offering to "defend the right of public school teachers to free speech both inside and outside the classroom, and explicitly adopted AAUP's conception of academic freedom."[3] In its own descriptions of attempts at stifling free speech, the ACLU broadened the list of topics from those covered by the AAUP to include antievolution laws, together with laws against other unpopular ideas, and also extended its scope to protect teachers in secondary education. It offered to assist in the defense of people in both schools and colleges who were accused in such cases.

The explosive combination of conflicting views was now firmly in place, and the fuse was lit when on March 21, 1925, the governor of Tennessee signed into law the Butler Act, which stated that it was

> AN ACT prohibiting the teaching of the Evolution Theory in all the Universities, Normals and all other public schools of Tennessee, which are supported in whole or in part by the public school funds of the State, and to provide penalties for the violations thereof.
>
> Section 1. *Be it enacted by the General Assembly of the State of Tennessee,* That it shall be unlawful for any teacher in any of the Universities, Normals and all other public schools of the State which are supported in whole or in part by the public school funds of the State, to teach any theory that denies the story of the Divine Creation of man as taught in the Bible, and to teach instead that man has descended from a lower order of animals.
>
> Section 2. *Be it further enacted,* That any teacher found guilty of the violation of this Act, Shall be guilty of a misdemeanor and upon conviction, shall be fined not less than One Hundred ($100.00) Dollars nor more than Five Hundred ($500.00) Dollars for each offense.

The ACLU, which had been following the progress of such legislation across the nation, decided to see if the Butler Act could be used as a test case and published a statement in the Tennessee papers on May 4, 1925, offering to defend any teacher prosecuted under the act.

When word got around about the ACLU press release seeking someone willing to test the law barring the teaching of evolution, some enterprising entrepreneurs in Dayton, Tennessee, saw in the ACLU's offer a golden opportunity to put their sleepy little town on the national map.

This set into rapid motion the sequence of events that led to the Scopes trial.

NOTES

1. Edward J. Larson, *Summer for the Gods* (Cambridge, MA: Harvard University Press, 1997), 64.

2. Larson, *Summer for the Gods*, 77.

3. Larson, *Summer for the Gods*, 81.

Chapter 5

The Scopes Pregame Show

Although the play and film *Inherit the Wind* based on the Scopes trial was made as a drama, the actual events leading up to and during the trial could just as well have been portrayed as a comedy.

Right from the beginning, rather than being a bitter adversarial contest between science and religion that tore apart a small town, the arrest and prosecution were staged by the civic leaders of Dayton mainly as a public relations exercise to benefit the town by increasing its visibility through publicity. They felt that a show trial, hopefully involving well-known national figures arguing a controversial topic that was being debated across the country and generating immense passions, would draw national media and tourists to the city, leading to an economic boom. So they quickly set about making sure that the trial took place in their town.

Dayton resident George Rappleyea, who personally opposed the antievolution Butler Act, worked with Fred Robinson (a local businessman and also chair of the county school board), the school superintendent (who supported the law), two city attorneys who agreed to prosecute the case, and a local attorney to handle the defense to put all the ingredients into place.[1]

All they needed now was someone to charge with violating the Butler Act. They did not want anyone's life or career to be harmed by what was essentially a publicity-seeking event. The team looked around for a suitable candidate to accuse and found one in twenty-four-year-old John T. Scopes, an easy-going general science instructor and part-time football coach. Although he was not the regular biology teacher, he made a good candidate because he was single

Mencken Finds Daytonians Full of Sickening Doubts about Value of Publicity

by H. L. Mencken

Dayton, Tenn., July 9.—On the eve of the great contest Dayton is full of sickening surges and tremors of doubt. Five or six weeks ago, when the infidel Scopes was first laid by the heels, there was no uncertainty in all this smiling valley. The town boomers leaped to the assault as one man. Here was an unexampled, almost a miraculous chance to get Dayton upon the front pages, to make it talked about, to put it upon the map. But how now?

Today, with the curtain barely rung up and the worst buffooneries to come, it is obvious to even town boomers that getting upon the map, like patriotism, is not enough. The getting there must be managed discreetly, adroitly, with careful regard to psychological niceties. The boomers of Dayton, alas, had no skill at such things, and the experts they called in were all quacks. The result now turns the communal liver to water. Two months ago the town was obscure and happy. Today it is a universal joke. . . .

The town, I confess, greatly surprised me. I expected to find a squalid Southern village, with darkies snoozing on the horse-blocks, pigs rooting under the houses and the inhabitants full of hookworm and malaria. What I found was a country town full of charm and even beauty—a somewhat smallish but nevertheless very attractive Westminster or Balair.

The houses are surrounded by pretty gardens, with cool green lawns and stately trees. The two chief streets are paved from curb to curb. The stores carry good stocks and have a metropolitan air, especially the drug, book, magazine, sporting goods and soda-water emporium of the estimable Robinson. A few of the town ancients still affect galluses and string ties, but the younger bucks are very nattily turned out. Scopes himself, even in his shirt sleeves, would fit into any college campus in America save that of Harvard alone.

Nor is there any evidence in the town of that poisonous spirit which usually shows itself when Christian men gather to defend the great doctrine of their faith. . . . On the contrary, the Evolutionists and the Anti-Evolutionists seem to be on the best of terms, and it is hard in a group to distinguish one from another. . . .

Rhea county, in fact, is proud of its tolerance, and apparently with good reason. The klan has never got a foothold here, though it rages everywhere else in Tennessee. When the first kleagles came in they got the cold shoulder, and pretty soon they gave up the county as hopeless. It is run today not by anonymous daredevils in white nightshirts, but by well-heeled Free-masons in decorous white aprons. In Dayton alone there are sixty thirty-second-degree Masons—an immense quota for so small a town. They believe in keeping the peace, and so even the stray Catholics of the town are treated politely, though everyone naturally regrets they are required to report to the Pope once a week.

It is probably this unusual tolerance, and not any extraordinary passion for the integrity of Genesis, that has made Dayton the scene of a celebrated case, and got its name upon the front pages, and caused its forward-looking men to begin to wonder uneasily if all advertising is really good advertising. . . .

Thus the battle joins and the good red sun shines down. Dayton lies in a fat and luxuriant valley. The bottoms are green with corn, pumpkins and young orchards and the hills are full of reliable moonshiners, all save one of them Christian men. . . . The fences are in good repair. The roads

(continued)

> are smooth and hard. The scene is set for a high-toned and
> even somewhat swagger combat. When it is over all the
> participants save Bryan will shake hands.
>
> —From H. L. Mencken, *Baltimore Sun*, July 10, 1925

and not a local and had no ties to the region or intention of staying
permanently in Dayton; thus, he had little to lose from the case. This
made him preferable to the married regular biology teacher, who
was also the school principal and thus had a lot more at stake.

In the film *Inherit the Wind*, Scopes was arrested in his classroom
by grim-faced city leaders while in the very act of teaching his class
about evolution, then flung into jail. While there, he had to listen to
hostile citizens marching around the jail carrying banners and chant-
ing slogans vilifying him, flinging bottles through his cell windows,
and burning him in effigy, while in the evening the local clergyman
preached fiery sermons condemning him to hell for his evil act.

In reality, Scopes was a cheerful coconspirator in the staged
trial. The chummy nature of the whole proceeding is illustrated by
the fact that all these friendly discussions took place in the local
drugstore owned by the school board chair. The prosecutor, who
happened to be Scopes's close friend, said he would be willing to
prosecute Scopes as long as Scopes didn't mind. Even during the
heat of the trial, the prosecutors and the defendant went for a swim
in a pond during a lunch recess.

Scopes was invited to these discussions and asked whether he
was agreeable to being prosecuted. Scopes believed in evolution and
disagreed with the law, so he said he was willing to go along. The
group then called over the waiting justice of the peace to swear out
a warrant for Scopes, and the waiting constable served it to him immediately. Rather than being flung into jail, Scopes then went off to
play tennis while the others set in motion the publicity machine by
wiring the state's newspapers with the news that they had charged
someone with violating the Butler Act.[2]

The little secret behind the trial was that it was never firmly established that Scopes had even taught evolution at all and thus actually
violated the law. He himself could not definitely recall teaching that
particular topic. He never took the stand in his defense and thus was

not forced to swear under oath on this issue. He and his students also seemed hazy on the entire concept of evolution. But everyone, including Scopes, decided to go along with the idea that he had taught it in order that the trial could take place.

Since Scopes had filled in occasionally when the regular biology teacher was absent and had used the assigned textbook, which included a section on human evolution, this was enough for the friendly gang of conspirators to decide that they could reasonably charge him with violating the law.[3] (During the later grand jury proceedings, Scopes even had to urge his reluctant students to testify against him and coached them on how to answer in order that the grand jury would have grounds to indict him.)

Thus, from the beginning, the normal antagonism that characterizes the two opposing sides in highly charged trials was absent. It was rumored that the ACLU, eager to have a test case on the issue of freedom of speech in the classroom, even volunteered to pay the expenses of the *prosecution*, but the offer was declined.

The generosity was not all on one side. Antievolutionist William Jennings Bryan had not even wanted a penalty provision inserted into the law since he only wanted to make a point about what should be taught, and he did not want to actually harm anyone, financially or otherwise. In fact, Bryan later offered, if Scopes were to be found guilty, to pay the fine himself, unlike in the film, where an outraged Bryan wanted a stiff sentence meted out.

Everyone fully expected Scopes to be found guilty, and even the defense hoped for such a verdict so that the case could be appealed to the higher courts, the constitutional issues more fully addressed, and wider precedents set. The Scopes trial in Dayton was to be merely the first act in a drama that was supposed to have much broader implications.

Once Scopes was charged with violating the Butler Act and the action was publicized, things started moving extremely rapidly.

On May 9, 1925, "the county's three justices of the peace formally held Scopes for action by the August grand jury, in the meantime releasing him without bond."[4] In mid May, the sixty-five-year-old William Jennings Bryan, who had been campaigning across the nation against the teaching of evolution, volunteered to appear for the prosecution for free, thus guaranteeing, to the city leaders' delight, that the trial would get the national publicity the instigators eagerly sought.

The local civic leaders, eager to get as many headliners as possible involved, even tried to get famous English author H. G. Wells, a supporter of evolution, to make the case for evolution at the trial. They considered that his distinguished literary presence would lend a certain cachet to the proceedings, but unfortunately for them, Wells declined to get involved.[5]

Fearing that other cities, belatedly realizing that holding a nationally prominent trial would generate a business boom, would try to take the spotlight away from Dayton by staging their own trials, the local leaders decided not to wait until the scheduled August date but to move even more quickly. So the district judge, "acting with the consent of both prosecution and defense, called a special session of the grand jury for May 25 to indict Scopes before any other town could steal the show."[6]

When attorney and well-known agnostic Clarence Darrow was initially approached about whether he would defend Scopes, he declined the offer because he had just retired at the age of sixty-eight and was not interested in taking on new cases. But when he heard that Bryan was appearing for the prosecution, the agnostic Darrow changed his mind and offered to appear on Scopes's behalf for no fee, relishing the chance to argue on a national stage against one of the most visible proponents of religion.

Darrow's involvement caused some dismay to the ACLU, which was underwriting the defense case. The organization wanted to focus the case on the issue of academic freedom and felt that Darrow's militant agnosticism would alienate otherwise sympathetic potential religious allies. But Scopes chose Darrow to be his lawyer and stuck with him, feeling that a wily and experienced defense lawyer was better than the constitutional lawyers that the ACLU preferred.[7]

Clarence Darrow (1857–1938) was the son of ardent abolitionists and supporters of women's suffrage. He became one of the foremost criminal lawyers of his time, the defense lawyer in the sensational Leopold and Loeb case, a strong defender of civil liberties, an opponent of the death penalty, a leading member of the ACLU, and a well-known scorner of religious beliefs.

William Jennings Bryan (1860–1925) was a lawyer who was elected to Congress from Nebraska in 1890 and 1892 but lost the race for the U.S. Senate in 1894. He was the Democratic nominee for president in 1896, 1900, and 1908, losing all three times, and was secretary of state in President Woodrow Wilson's administration from 1913 until 1915. He was a populist, a peace activist, an anti-imperialist, and a Prohibitionist.

Clarence Darrow was the perfect foil for William Jennings Bryan. Although famous for his successful defenses in several high-profile criminal cases, Darrow also "delighted in challenging traditional concepts of morality and religion." He called himself an agnostic but was effectively an atheist, in which respect he was very similar to Charles Darwin. According to Darrow's biographer, "He regarded Christianity as a 'slave religion,' encouraging acquiescence in injustice, a willingness to make do with the mediocre, and complacency in the face of the intolerable."[8] Edward J. Larson writes,

> Good intentions underlay Darrow's efforts to undermine popular religious faith. He sincerely believed that the biblical concept of original sin for all and salvation for some through divine grace was, as he described it, "a very dangerous doctrine"—"silly, impossible, and wicked." Darrow once told a group of convicts, "It is not the bad people I fear so much as the good people. When a person is sure that he is good, he is nearly hopeless; he gets cruel—he believes in punishment." During a public debate on religion, he added, "The origin of what we call civilization is not due to religion but to skepticism. . . . The modern world is the child of doubt and inquiry, as the ancient world was the child of fear and faith. . . ."
>
> Darrow readily embraced the antitheistic implications of Darwinism.[9]

Since both Bryan and Darrow were itching to square off against each other on the grand issue of science and religion, it was almost guaranteed that the trial would extend well beyond issues of free speech. The stage was now set for a trial that would reverberate across the nation and color all future discussions on this topic.

The trial aroused so much national and worldwide interest that the rural courtroom was wired with the latest technology, using every possible means to broadcast the proceedings immediately to the world. There were a telegraph and telephone, a movie newsreel camera, and radio microphones that sent live coverage to WGN Radio in Chicago, which in turn rebroadcast the trial live over a national network. This was the first such national live broadcast of a trial. Considering that the charged offense was a mere misdemeanor, this extraordinary media blitz shows how the underlying issues captured everyone's imagination.

Interestingly, the Scopes case was really fought on two levels, both of which have continued to this day.

The surface level dealt with legal and political questions about what could and could not be taught in public schools and who was entitled to make that determination. The lead prosecutor, state attorney general Tom Stewart, wanted to try the case on a simple question of fact: whether Scopes had violated the law by teaching about human evolution. Hence, he opposed the introduction of any scientific expert testimony on the merits of evolution or any biblical analysis, arguing that these were irrelevant.

Meanwhile, his co-counsel, Bryan, was arguing two other points: (1) that the community, through its elected representatives, had the right to decide what should be taught in the local schools, and (2) that since the teaching of religious doctrines had already been eliminated from public schools, so should other unproven doctrines like evolution, especially since the latter doctrine undermined the former. As he wrote in his essay "God and Evolution"[10] (the first paragraph of which was quoted before in chapter 3),

> The Bible has in many places been excluded from the schools on the ground that religion should not be taught by those paid by public taxation. If this doctrine is sound, what right have the enemies of religion to teach irreligion in the public schools? If the Bible cannot be taught, why should Christian taxpayers permit the teaching of guesses that make the Bible a lie? . . .
>
> Our opponents are not fair. When we find fault with the teaching of Darwin's unsupported hypothesis, they talk about Copernicus and Galileo and ask whether we shall exclude science and return to the dark ages. Their evasion is a confession of weakness. We do not ask for the exclusion of any scientific truth, but we do protest against an atheist teacher being allowed to blow his guesses in the face of the student. The

Christians who want to teach religion in their schools furnish the money for denominational institutions. If atheists want to teach atheism, why do they not build their own schools and employ their own teachers?

Bryan was trying to drive a wedge between what he considered well-established scientific truths (like the heliocentric model of the solar system) and unproven theories like evolution. Bryan was also advocating a majoritarian point of view, arguing that elected officials had the right to determine what was taught and to exclude those things that were not scientific facts.

Darrow and the ACLU for the defense were arguing that this was an issue of academic freedom, that teachers should not be barred by law from teaching what they believed to be true.[11]

Their main strategy was to exploit the fact that the wording in the Butler Act only prohibited teaching evolution that "denies the story of the Divine Creation of man as taught in the Bible." This provided them with an opening to examine the role that interpretation played in understanding the message of the Bible and to show that more sophisticated interpretations seemed to make the Bible and evolution compatible.

This line of argument provided them with an opportunity to explain to the court the theory of evolution, to show that it was so well established that it had the widespread support of scientists, and to argue that teachers should have the free speech right to teach accepted scientific theories without the threat of punishment. This strategy led them to request that they be allowed to provide the expert testimony of scientists and theologians.

But beneath these surface-level arguments, there was clearly another level: both Bryan and Darrow thought that the theory of evolution and religion did conflict and that one had to be right and the other wrong. This was the real fight relished and sought by both, the fight to determine which worldview was true.

Bryan felt that applying the ideas of evolution to human beings led to a devaluation of humanity and was the cause of much evil in the world. Being a political progressive and advocate of peace, he was concerned that the theory of evolution was leading to exploitation, injustice, and war. He was thus eager to argue a much more expansive case and show that evolution was a false and dangerous theory.

Darrow was a well-known militant agnostic who thought that Christianity was just a bunch of superstitions and relished the chance to demonstrate the absurdity of Christian beliefs and the superiority of science.

This second front in the case caused some consternation for both men's legal allies, who felt that it was a distraction. But with the two most famous people involved in the case both eager to extend it not only beyond narrow questions of fact but also beyond the issue of free speech, it was inevitable that they would prevail and the case would become a high-profile contest between evolution and religion, just as the civic leaders in Dayton had hoped.

The legal backdrop to the Scopes case did not involve the U.S. Constitution. The First Amendment to the Constitution (ratified as part of the Bill of Rights on December 15, 1791) reads, "Congress shall make no law respecting an establishment of religion, or prohibiting the free exercise thereof; or abridging the freedom of speech, or of the press; or the right of the people peaceably to assemble, and to petition the Government for a redress of grievances." It is important to realize that originally the First Amendment was considered to apply only to laws passed by the *federal* government since the wording explicitly only barred *Congress* from passing any law that infringed on those rights.

It was the Fourteenth Amendment dealing with civil rights (adopted on July 9, 1868, following the end of the Civil War) that started the expansion of the scope of the Bill of Rights. This amendment said, among other things, "No State shall make or enforce any law which shall abridge the privileges or immunities of citizens of the United States; nor shall any State deprive any person of life, liberty, or property, without due process of law; nor deny to any person within its jurisdiction the equal protection of the laws."

The use of the more expansive word "state" instead of "Congress" in the due process clause resulted in subsequent U.S. Supreme Court cases expanding the reach of the due process, equal protection, and life, liberty, or property clauses of the Fourteenth Amendment to cover the First Amendment, protecting those freedoms from encroachment by state government agencies as well.

The first expansive reading of this sort occurred a month before the Scopes trial on June 8, 1925, when, in *Gitlow v. New York*,[12] the Supreme Court asserted that the First Amendment freedoms of speech and the press were two of the liberties protected from infringement by state and local governments under the Fourteenth Amendment. The court said in its opinion, "For present purposes, we may and do assume that freedom of speech and of the press which are protected by the First Amendment from abridgment by Congress are among the fundamental personal rights and "liberties" protected by the due process clause of the Fourteenth Amendment from impairment by the States."

Eventually, by a series of these kinds of expansions, all Bill of Rights protections were extended so that they could not be encroached upon even by state or local governments or, indeed, any body acting as an agent of the government. But that was some way down the road, occurring long after the Scopes trial. The *Gitlow* verdict, delivered just a month before the Scopes case went to trial, came too late to be included as part of the strategy of the Scopes defense team. They chose to argue on the basis of free speech under the Tennessee state constitution rather than the federal one.

NOTES

1. Edward J. Larson, *Summer for the Gods* (Cambridge, MA: Harvard University Press, 1997), 89–91.

2. Larson, *Summer for the Gods*, 91.

3. Larson, *Summer for the Gods*, 108.

4. Larson, *Summer for the Gods*, 95.

5. Larson, *Summer for the Gods*, 96.

6. Larson, *Summer for the Gods*, 96.

7. Larson, *Summer for the Gods*, 102.

8. Larson, *Summer for the Gods*, 71.

9. Larson, *Summer for the Gods*, 71.

10. William Jennings Bryan, "God and Evolution," *New York Times*, February 26, 1922, 84.

11. Note that this is an interesting reversal of recent battles where it is the advocates of creationism who argue that not allowing the teaching of intelligent design in schools violates the free speech rights of teachers. As we will see later, this switch has occurred because, as a result of several U.S. Supreme Court decisions, the legal and constitutional issues involved have shifted considerably from those that were at issue in the Scopes trial.

12. *Gitlow v. New York*, 268 U.S. 652 (1925), www.law.cornell.edu/supct/html/historics/USSC_CR_0268_0652_ZO.html.

Chapter 6

The Scopes Trial

The Scopes trial has cast such a long shadow and reverberated so much in public consciousness that it is worthwhile to quickly summarize the events of the trial in order to separate the facts from the folklore that has arisen around it as a result of *Inherit the Wind*.[1]

The trial itself was brief, lasting just eight days, much of it involving wrangling over legal technicalities that took place with the jury out of the courtroom. On only two occasions were William Jennings Bryan and Clarence Darrow able to make speeches, and these occurred in the middle of the trial during legal skirmishes.

Day 1, Friday, July 10: The morning saw the grand jury and witnesses appear to issue a new indictment since the older one was discovered to have had a technical flaw. John Scopes had to tell a reluctant student that he would be doing him a favor by testifying against him and then was duly indicted again. After lunch, jury selection took place.

Day 2, Monday, July 13: The defense moved to quash the indictment on the grounds that it violated, among other things, the Tennessee state constitution's guarantee of individual freedom of speech and religion. The defense expected this to be overruled (and it was) but needed to file the motion in order to use these grounds to appeal to the higher courts later. The defense also argued that the theory of evolution was as well established as the Copernican theory; thus, to forbid teaching it was an unreasonable action by the state. The prosecution countered with the majoritarian view that the state had the right to prohibit the teaching of any subject at all.[2]

Impossibility of Obtaining Fair Jury Insures Scopes' Conviction, Says Mencken

by H. L. Mencken

Dayton, Tenn., July 10.—It may seem fabulous, but it is a sober fact that a sound Episcopalian or even a Northern Methodist would be regarded as virtually an atheist in Dayton. Here the only genuine conflict is between true believers. . . . To call a man a doubter in these parts is equal to accusing him of cannibalism. . . .

The selection of a jury to try Scopes, which went on all yesterday afternoon in the atmosphere of a blast furnace, showed to what extreme lengths the salvation of the local primates has been pushed. It was obvious after a few rounds that the jury would be unanimously hot for Genesis. The most that Mr. Darrow could hope for was to sneak in a few bold enough to declare publicly that they would have to hear the evidence against Scopes before condemning him. . . . Once a man was challenged without examination for simply admitting that he did not belong formally to any church. Another time a panel man who confessed that he was prejudiced against evolution got a hearty round of applause from the crowd. . . .

In brief this is a strictly Christian community, and such is its notion of fairness, justice and due process of law. . . . Its people are simply unable to imagine a man who rejects the literal authority of the Bible.

—From *Baltimore Evening Sun*, July 11, 1925

Then, Clarence Darrow rose to give what some say was the best speech of his long career. He pointed out that Tennessee had been teaching about evolution for years with no problem until people like Bryan came along and tried to use the Bible to determine what should or should not be taught. He said the new law made the Bible the yard stick to measure every man's intellect, to measure every man's intelligence, and to measure every man's learning. . . . The state of Tennessee under an honest and fair interpretation of the constitution has no more right to teach the Bible as the divine book than that the Koran is one, or the book of Mormon, or the book of Confucius, or the Buddha, or the Essays of Emerson. . . . There is nothing else, your Honor, that has caused the difference of opinion, of bitterness, of hatred, of war, of cruelty, that religion has caused.

His statement provided a rousing finish to the day.

Day 3, Tuesday, July 14: This day saw some legal wrangling over the propriety of having opening prayers at such a trial and an investigation by the judge over the source of some leaks of his anticipated ruling on whether to quash the indictment and dismiss the charges. It turned out that the judge himself was inadvertently responsible for the leak.

Darrow's Eloquent Appeal Wasted on Ears That Heed Only Bryan, Says Mencken

by H. L. Mencken

Dayton, Tenn., July 14.—During the whole time of [Clarence Darrow's speech], the old mountebank, Bryan, sat tight-lipped and unmoved. There is, of course, no reason why it should have shaken him. He has those hill billies locked up in his pen and he knows it. His brand is on them. He is at home among them. Since his earliest days, indeed, his chief strength has been among the folk of remote hills and forlorn and lonely farms. Now with his political aspirations all gone to pot, he turns to them for religious consolations. They understand his peculiar imbecilities. His nonsense is their ideal of sense. When he deluges them with his theological bilge they rejoice like pilgrims disporting in the river Jordan.

—From *Baltimore Evening Sun*, July 14, 1925

Day 4, Wednesday, July 15: The judge, as expected, rejected the motion to quash the indictment, and the trial proper got under way. The prosecution's opening statement consisted of just two sentences saying merely that they would show that Scopes had violated the law by teaching that "mankind is descended from a lower order of animals" and that therefore "he has taught a theory which denies the divine creation of man as taught in the Bible."

The defense said in its opening statement, "We will show by the testimony of men learned in science and theology that there are millions of people who believe in evolution and in the story of creation as set forth in the Bible and who find no conflict between the two. The defense maintains that this is a matter of faith and interpretation, which each individual must make for himself."[3]

The prosecution called only four witnesses. The school superintendent testified that the official school textbook did refer to evolution and that Scopes had admitted to teaching it. Two students testified that Scopes had taught them evolution, and the chair of the local school board (in whose drugstore the whole plan for this trial had been hatched) testified that Scopes had admitted to him that he had taught evolution. The prosecution completed its case in less than an hour.

The defense began by calling zoologist Maynard Metcalf of Johns Hopkins University, who was himself religious, to provide expert testimony on evolution. Metcalf distinguished between the *fact* of evolution having occurred, which he said scientists accepted, and the *theory* behind it, about which he said there were still some unanswered questions.

Day 5, Thursday, July 16: The day began with a debate about whether further expert testimony on evolution should be allowed. Bryan gave a rousing two-hour speech, the only one he made at the trial, although he gave many speeches outside the courtroom during that period. In his speech, he recapitulated many of the points described earlier in his 1922 *New York Times* essay.

Dudley Fields Malone, a member of the defense team, responded to this with an equally rousing speech, saying that the defense wanted a chance to prove the truth of evolution and the benefits of science. "We feel we stand with science. We feel we stand with intelligence. We feel we stand with fundamental freedom in America. We are not afraid."[4]

Although chief prosecutor Tom Stewart had wanted to stick to just the facts of the case, Malone's speech compelled him to clarify exactly where he stood on the big question of science versus religion. He ended the day with a dramatic speech in which he said that evolution "strikes at the very vitals of civilization and Christianity and is not entitled to a chance."[5] He also said, "They say it is a battle between religion and science. If it is, I want to serve notice now, in the name of the great God, that I am on the side of religion . . . because I want to know beyond this world that there might be an eternal happiness for me and for others."[6]

Day 6, Friday, July 17: The judge ruled on the issue of allowing further expert testimony by saying that the "defense could present written affidavits or read prepared statements into the record . . . but the prosecution could cross-examine any witness put on the stand."[7] This requirement posed a problem for the defense: they wanted to present expert testimony on the stand, but they feared that cross-examination would reveal that although their scientists were religious people, they did not believe in the literal truth of the virgin birth and other miracles.

As defense attorney Arthur Garfield Hays said, "It was felt by us that if the cause of free education was ever to be won, it would need the support of millions of intelligent churchgoing people who didn't question theological miracles," and that kind of testimony risked losing such support.[8] So the defense agreed to provide written affidavits to be entered into the record for the purposes of appellate review, and the trial adjourned for the weekend.

Over the weekend, eight scientists prepared written testimony essentially saying that "evolution is a fact, and that a well rounded education cannot well do without it."[9] Some sought to reconcile evolution with creation, as did four religion experts.[10] But while that preparation was going on, Darrow was planning the surprise that would forever after grab the imagination of the public and define the trial.

Day 7, Monday, July 20: In the Genesis account of creation, after six days spent in creating the universe, God rested. But in the Scopes trial, day seven was when the most dramatic activity occurred. It began quietly enough with the acceptance into the record of the written testimony prepared by experts over the weekend, along with a two-hour reading of excerpts by defense counsel Arthur Garfield Hays. All of this was kept from the jury. It was then that Darrow dropped his bombshell. He said that he would call the prosecutor William Jennings Bryan as a (hostile) witness for the defense in the afternoon.

Mencken Declares Strictly Fair Trial Is Beyond Ken of Tennessee Fundamentalists

by H. L. Mencken

Dayton, Tenn., July 16.—To these simple folk, as I have said, he [Bryan] is a prophet of the imperial line—a lineal successor to Moses and Abraham. The barbaric cosmogony that he believes in seems as reasonable to them as it does to him. They share his peasant-like suspicion of all book learning that a plow hand cannot grasp. They believe with him that men who know too much should be seized by the secular arm and put down by force. They dream as he does of a world unanimously sure of Heaven and unanimously idiotic on this earth.

This old buzzard, having failed to raise the mob against its rulers, now prepares to raise it against its teachers. He can never be the peasants' President, but there is still a chance to be the peasants' Pope. He leads a new crusade, his bald head glistening, his face streaming with sweat, his chest heaving beneath his rumpled alpaca coat. One somehow pities him, despite his so palpable imbecilities. It is a tragedy, indeed, to begin life as a hero and to end it as a buffoon. But let no one, laughing at him, underestimate the magic that lies in his black, malignant eye, his frayed but still eloquent voice. He can shake and inflame these poor ignoramuses as no other man among us can shake and inflame them, and he is desperately eager to order the charge.

In Tennessee he is drilling his army. The big battles, he believes, will be fought elsewhere.

—From *Baltimore Evening Sun*, July 16, 1925.

Battle Now Over, Mencken Sees; Genesis Triumphant and Ready for New Jousts

by H. L. Mencken

Dayton, Tenn., July 18.—All that remains of the great cause of the State of Tennessee against the infidel Scopes is the formal business of bumping off the defendant. There may be some legal jousting on Monday and some gaudy oratory on Tuesday, but the main battle is over, with Genesis completely triumphant. Judge Raulston finished the benign business yesterday morning by leaping with soft judicial hosannas into the arms of the prosecution. The sole commentary of the sardonic Darrow consisted of bringing down a metaphorical custard pie upon the occiput of the learned jurist. . . .

Darrow has lost this case. It was lost long before he came to Dayton. But it seems to me that he has nevertheless performed a great public service by fighting it to a finish and in a perfectly serious way. Let no one mistake it for comedy, farcical though it may be in all its details. It serves notice on the country that Neanderthal man is organizing in these forlorn backwaters of the land, led by a fanatic, rid sense and devoid of conscience. Tennessee, challenging him too timorously and too late, now sees its courts converted into camp meetings and its Bill of Rights made a mock of by its sworn officers of the law. There are other States that had better look to their arsenals before the Hun is at their gates.

—From *Baltimore Evening Sun*, July 18, 1925.

Although the rest of the prosecution team saw no good coming from this highly unusual request and objected, Bryan relished the opportunity to have a verbal duel with Darrow, to fight for God and Christianity against the militant agnostic, and said he would testify, provided he could put the defense team on the stand as well.

Finally, the clash of titans the entire nation following the trial had been waiting for was about to occur. When word got around of what was going to happen that day after lunch, huge crowds gathered to see the spectacle, and the judge had to order that the trial be moved outdoors to accommodate the onlookers, partly because of the sweltering heat indoors and partly because he feared the floor would collapse under their weight. Bryan took the stand for the defense on Monday afternoon, and the rest, as they say, is history.

Bryan's testimony did not go well. The film *Inherit the Wind*, in an extended and gripping climactic scene, captures what happened quite accurately. While Bryan could hold his own in grand debates over the big ideas of evolution and religion, the constraints of being a witness in a court case worked against him because the scope of his responses was limited by the questions that Darrow chose.

Darrow did not ask the kinds of questions that would allow Bryan to make sweeping statements on the nature of science, humans, God, the soul, and evolution. Instead he pressed him on very narrowly focused topics based on specific assertions made in the Bible:[11] Did Jonah actually live in the whale for three days? How could Joshua lengthen the day by "stopping the Sun" when it is the Earth rotating about its own axis that causes day and night? When did the great flood occur? How old is the Earth? Do you believe the first woman was Eve? Do you believe she was made from Adam's rib? If the serpent in the Garden of Eden was compelled to crawl on its belly as punishment for tempting Adam and Eve, how did it move about before that? Did it walk on its tail? Where did Cain get his wife? And so on.

None of these questions had anything to do with human evolution, but they challenged Bryan to defend a literal interpretation of the Bible and put him in a quandary. If Bryan stuck to the literal truth of the Bible in every detail, Darrow could make him look ridiculous by showing him to be completely out of touch with modern ideas and a prisoner of medieval thinking, thus discrediting the entire fundamentalist movement.

If Bryan denied the literal truth and allowed for interpretation of at least some parts of the Bible as metaphors, then he weakened

Excerpts from Clarence Darrow's Questioning of William Jennings Bryan

Darrow: How long ago was the Flood, Mr. Bryan?

Bryan: Let me see Ussher's calculation about it. . . . It is given here, as 2348 years B.C.

D: Well, 2348 years B.C. You believe that all the living things that were not contained in the ark were destroyed?

B: I think the fish may have lived.

D: Outside of the fish?

B: I cannot say.

D: You cannot say?

B: No, except that just as it is, I have no proof to the contrary.

D: I am asking whether you believe?

B: I do.

D: That all living things outside of the fish were destroyed?

B: What I say about the fish is merely a matter of humor.

. . .

D: You are not satisfied there is any civilization that can be traced back 5,000 years?

B: I would not want to say there is because I have no evidence of it that is satisfactory.

. . .

D: Let me make this definite. You believe that every civilization on the earth and every living thing, except possibly the fishes, that came out of the ark were wiped out by the Flood?

B: At that time.

(continued)

D: At that time. And then, whatever human beings, including all the tribes, that inhabited the world, and have inhabited the world, and who run their pedigree straight back, and all the animals, have come onto the earth since the Flood?

B: Yes.

D: Within 4,200 years. Do you know a scientific man on the face of the earth that believes any such thing?

B: I cannot say, but I know some scientific men who dispute entirely the antiquity of man as testified to by other scientific men.

D: Oh, that does not answer the question. Do you know of a single scientific man on the face of the earth that believes any such thing as you stated, about the antiquity of man.

B: I don't think I have ever asked one the direct question.

D: Quite important, isn't it?

B: Well, I don't know as it is.

D: It might not be?

B: If I had nothing else to do except speculate on what our remote ancestors were and what our remote descendants have been, but I have been more interested in Christians going on right now, to make it much more important than speculation on either the past or the future.

D: You have never had any interest in the age of the various races and people and civilization and animals that exist upon the earth today? Is that right?

B: I have never felt a great deal of interest in the effort that has been made to dispute the Bible by the speculations of men, or the investigations of men.

. . .

D: You do know that there are thousands of people who profess to be Christians who believe the earth is much more ancient and that the human race is much more ancient?

B: I think there may be.

D: And you have never investigated to find out how long man has been on the earth?

B: I have never found it necessary.

D: For any reason, whatever it is?

B: To examine every speculation; but if I had done it I never would have done anything else.

D: I ask for a direct answer.

B: I do not expect to find out all those things, and I do not expect to find out about races.

D: I didn't ask you that. Now, I ask you if you know if it was interesting enough, or important enough for you to try and find out about how old these ancient civilizations were?

B: No; I have not made a study of it.

D: Don't you know that the ancient civilizations of China are 6,000 or 7,000 years old, at the very least?

B: No; but they would not run back beyond the creation, according to the Bible, 6,000 years.

. . .

D: You have never in all your life made any attempt to find out about the other peoples of the earth—how old their civilizations are—how long they had existed on the earth, have you?

B: No sir, I have been so well satisfied with the Christian religion, that I have spent no time trying to find arguments against it.

D: Were you afraid you might find some?

B: No, sir. I am not afraid now that you will show me any . . . . I have all the information I want to live by and to die by.

D: And that's all you are interested in?

(*continued*)

B: I am not looking more on any religion.

D: You don't care how old the earth is, how old man is, and how long the animals have been here?

B: I am not so much interested in that.

D: You have never made any investigation to find out?

B: No, sir, I have never.

D: All right.

. . .

D: Do you believe that the first woman was Eve?

B: Yes.

D: Do you believe she was literally made out of Adam's rib?

B: I do.

D: Did you ever discover where Cain got his wife?

B: No sir; I leave the agnostics to hunt for her.

D: You have never found out?

B: I have never tried to find.

D: You have never tried to find?

B: No.

D: The Bible says he got one, doesn't he? Were there other people on the earth at that time?

B: I cannot say.

D: You cannot say. Did that ever enter your consideration?

B: Never bothered me.

D: There were no others recorded, but Cain got a wife.

B: That's what the Bible says.

D: Where she came from you do not know. All right.

—From the trial transcripts in Jeffrey P. Moran, *The Scopes Trial: A Brief History with Documents*, 2002.

the prosecution's case since the defense was arguing that the law only forbade the teaching of "any theory that denies the story of the Divine Creation of man as taught in the Bible." Since modernist theologians had said that the Bible could be interpreted so that it was compatible with evolution, the defense could argue that Scopes had not violated the law since there was no way of saying for certain what the Bible said about creation.

Even some modernist theologians and religious scientists who opposed Bryan's crusade against evolution criticized Darrow's line of questioning because it was based on old-fashioned views of Christianity and seemed designed mostly to make Bryan look foolish. They felt that if Darrow wanted to explore the important philosophical issues in the evolution-religion debate, he should have based his questions on a more sophisticated understanding of the Bible.

But it is likely that Darrow, canny and experienced trial lawyer that he was, knew exactly what he was doing. He had zeroed in on his opponent's weakest point. He must have known that religion is at its strongest when it is making grand, sweeping statements on the nature of life and the universe, because those are vague and hard to pin down or contradict. It is at its weakest when trying to explain concrete and specific details.

Under Darrow's questioning, Bryan faced the same problem that religious people have to this day. It is easy to proclaim faith in grand beliefs, but when it comes to specifics like Noah's flood or the story of Jonah or a woman being created from Adam's rib, it becomes harder to explain how such particulars could possibly be literally true and, if they are not, why you should believe some things in the Bible and not others. As Darrow said later, his strategy was meant to force Bryan to "choose between crude beliefs and the common intelligence of modern times . . . or to admit ignorance."[12]

Confronted with Darrow's relentless examination focused on such narrow issues, Bryan chose the option of pleading ignorance, saying that he was not interested in finding answers to the questions posed by Darrow and thus could not answer them, although he believed that, for God, all things were possible and that answers would be forthcoming some day. In other words, he resorted to that faithful old religious standby, the "mysterious ways clause," which attributes all seemingly inexplicable phenomena to the actions of an inscrutable God.

Questions Darrow Might Ask Bryan Today

If the trial took place with today's scientific knowledge, Darrow might have asked the following questions in the same vein: If Jesus was conceived by a virgin, from where did he get his Y chromosome? Whose genetic information did it contain? How did Mary's egg get fertilized? If life begins at conception, as some claim, does the human soul enter that very first fertilized cell? When that first cell divides into two, what happens to the soul in it? Does it stay within the first cell, does it split in two, does it double, or does it somehow straddle the two cells? Since the majority of human embryos spontaneously abort, why does God cause that to happen? What happens to their souls, and why did God bother to give them souls in the first place if he was going to abort them later?

But since Bryan had said at the beginning of his testimony that he had studied the Bible deeply for fifty years, his repeatedly claiming to lack curiosity about such obvious questions and pleading ignorance of how to reconcile commonly known scientific facts that contradicted a literal reading of the Bible resulted in his coming across like an incurious know-nothing. This enabled Darrow to suggest that adopting Bryan's position on banning the teaching of evolution would be to condemn students to ignorance, in contrast to teaching them science, which advocated active curiosity and the search for answers.

When Darrow said during his questioning of Bryan, "You insult every man of science and learning in the world because he does [not] believe in your fool religion. . . . I am [examining] you on your fool ideas that no intelligent Christian on earth believes," he was not making his case to the jury but to the larger world.

And he succeeded. The next day's front-page *New York Times*[13] report on the trial reflects how badly Bryan fared under the questioning, so much so that even the Dayton spectators, who were his natural allies and had come to see their hero vanquish the skeptic Darrow, ended up laughing at him.

> So-called Fundamentalists of Tennessee sat under the trees of the Rhea County Court House lawn today listening to William J. Bryan defend his faith in the "literal truth" of the Bible, and laughed. . . .
>
> The greatest crowd of the trial had come in anticipation of hearing Messrs. Bryan and Darrow speak, and it got more than it expected. It saw Darrow and Bryan in actual conflict—Mr. Darrow's rationalism in combat with Mr. Bryan's faith—and forgot for the moment that Bryan's faith was its own. . . .
>
> To the crowd spread under the trees watching the amazing spectacle on the platform the fight seemed a fair one. There was no pity for the helplessness of the believer come so suddenly and so unexpectedly upon a moment when he could not reconcile statements of the Bible with generally accepted facts. There was no pity for his admissions of ignorance of things boys and girls learn in high school, his floundering confessions that he knew practically nothing of geology, biology, philology, little of comparative religion, and little even of ancient history.
>
> These Tennesseans were enjoying a fight. That an ideal of a great man, a biblical scholar, an authority on religion, was being dispelled seemed to make no difference. They grinned with amusement and expectation, until the next blow by one side or the other came, and then they guffawed again. And finally, when Mr. Bryan, pressed harder and harder by Mr. Darrow, confessed he did not believe everything in the Bible should be taken literally, the crowd howled.

The other members of the prosecuting team saw the damage being done by this line of questioning and repeatedly objected, but Bryan bravely, and perhaps foolishly, insisted on continuing until the trial adjourned for the day, saying that he did not want to be accused of fearing to answer questions. He also probably felt that he could repair any damage during his closing statement in the case, where he would have full rein to make the kind of grand arguments in favor of God and the Bible and against evolution that had proven so successful when he gave public speeches.

Day 8, Tuesday, July 21: The Scopes trial came to an abrupt end on the eighth day.

The judge began the proceedings by halting the questioning of Bryan and ordered his previous day's testimony stricken from the record. But the damage had already been done since the point of the case, after all, was not to persuade the jury in the room but to score points with a wider national audience. Darrow had exploited his questioning of Bryan to gain a major propaganda victory for science, in the full glare of the national media, by showing that religious beliefs like Bryan's led to an intellectual cul-de-sac.

Following the judge's ruling ending Bryan's testimony, the defense promptly rested its case, and Darrow made a brief statement asking the jury to bring in a verdict of *guilty*. The defense's strategy all along had been to argue against the Butler Act on constitutional grounds in the appellate courts. In order for there to be grounds for such an appeal, the lower court had to find Scopes guilty. Since pleading guilty at the outset would not have allowed Scopes to appeal, he had to plead innocent and yet be convicted, which explains the seemingly strange request of a defense counsel asking a jury for a guilty verdict against his own client. Darrow told the jury,

> As far as this case stands before the jury, the court has told you very plainly that if you think my client taught that man descended from a lower order of animals, you will find him guilty, and you heard the testimony of the boys on that questions and heard read [sic] the books, and there is no dispute about the facts. Scopes did not go on the stand, because he could not deny the statements made by the boys. I do not know how you may feel, I am not especially interested in it, but this case and this law will never be decided until it gets to a higher court, and it cannot get to a higher court probably, very well, unless you bring in a verdict.[14]

But there was an additional benefit to be gained by the defense's simply asking for a directed verdict of guilty and resting its case without presenting a closing statement. According to trial rules, this meant that the prosecution could not make a closing statement either. The defense was executing a deliberate strategy to prevent the prosecution, especially Bryan, from having the last word. So, rather than Bryan ending the case by making the kind of grand, eloquent, and sweeping speech that the Boy Orator was famous for, his final impression was his dismal performance on the witness stand. Darrow had outmaneuvered Bryan.

The jury duly complied with Darrow's request and, after just a few minutes of deliberation, returned with the verdict, finding Scopes guilty. The jury said they had not decided on the size of the penalty, and the judge said he would impose the minimum sentence required by law, which was $100. The chief prosecutor said that he thought that Tennessee law required the jury, not the judge, to set the fine, but the judge said it was his understanding that as long as it was just the minimum fine, he could set it, and all sides agreed to go along with this.

The case ended with both sides claiming victory.

Although the prosecution got its guilty verdict, the defense could claim that despite the inevitable, and even desired, legal loss, they had won the greater victory by showing the world the superiority of science over religion. As H. L. Mencken wrote at the time, "Darrow has lost this case. It was lost long before he came to Dayton. But it seems to me that he has nevertheless performed a great public service by fighting it to a finish and in a perfectly serious way. Let no one mistake it for comedy, farcical though it may be in all its details. It serves notice on the country that Neanderthal man is organizing in these forlorn backwaters of the land, led by a fanatic, rid sense and devoid of conscience."[15] And again, "Bryan went there in a hero's shining armor, bent deliberately upon a gross crime against sense. He came out a wrecked and preposterous charlatan, his tail between his legs. Few Americans have ever done so much for their country in a whole lifetime as Darrow did in two hours."[16]

The verdict was duly appealed to the higher courts, where the seemingly trivial bit of court business over who should decide the fine would result in the case not having the legal impact that had been sought.

NOTES

1. For a comprehensive review of the case, see Edward J. Larson, *Summer for the Gods* (Cambridge, MA: Harvard University Press, 1997). For a description of the trial and excerpts from the trial transcript, see Jeffrey P. Moran, *The Scopes Trial: A Brief History with Documents* (Boston: Bedford/St. Martins, 2002) and www.law.umkc.edu/faculty/projects/ftrials/scopes/scopes2.htm. To get a flavor of the atmosphere during the trial, read H. L. Mencken's account at www.law.umkc.edu/faculty/projects/ftrials/scopes/menk.htm. A timeline of the trial can be seen at www.antievolution.org/topics/law/scopes/scopes.html.

2. Larson, *Summer for the Gods*, 158–60.

3. Larson, *Summer for the Gods*, 171.

4. Larson, *Summer for the Gods*, 179.

5. Larson, *Summer for the Gods*, 180.

6. Larson, *Summer for the Gods*, 179.

7. Larson, *Summer for the Gods*, 181.

8. Larson, *Summer for the Gods*, 181.

9. Larson, *Summer for the Gods*, 184.

10. Larson, *Summer for the Gods*, 186.

11. For fascinating extracts from the transcript of the questions and answers, see Jeffrey P. Moran, *The Scopes Trial: A Brief History with Documents* (Boston: Bedford/St. Martins, 2002) and also www.law.umkc.edu/faculty/projects/ftrials/scopes/day7.htm.

12. Larson, *Summer for the Gods*, 188.

13. *New York Times*, "Big Crowd Watches Trial Under Trees: Applauds Bryan's Defense of the Bible and Laughs at Sallies of Darrow." July 21, 1925, 1.

14. See www.law.umkc.edu/faculty/projects/ftrials/scopes/day8.htm.

15. H. L. Mencken, "Battle Now Over, Mencken Sees; Genesis Triumphant and Ready for New Jousts," *Baltimore Evening Sun*, July 18, 1925, www.positiveatheism.org/hist/menck04.htm#SCOPESA.

16. H. L. Mencken, "Bryan," *Baltimore Evening Sun*, September 14, 1925, www.positiveatheism.org/hist/menck05.htm#SCOPESC.

Chapter 7

The Scopes Appeal

The *Scopes* verdict was appealed to the Tennessee Supreme Court. Many people on the defense side, including the ACLU, tried to have Clarence Darrow removed from the defense team for the appeal since they wanted to bring the focus back to the issue of free speech and feared that Darrow's strong antipathy toward religion would result in that issue dominating once again. But Darrow and his allies outmaneuvered them, and he stayed on.

The Tennessee Supreme Court heard oral arguments in May 1926. Many briefs were filed on both sides, with the state again arguing the majoritarian view that elected representatives' decisions were binding, whatever their merits, and basing its argument on a recent U.S. Supreme Court judgment upholding compulsory school vaccinations because of the public good. The lawyers for the state said, "What the public believes is for the common welfare must be accepted as tending to promote the common welfare whether it does in fact or not."[1]

The state also argued that the Butler Act was not designed to promote any sectarian religious belief but instead to level the playing field in education: since the Bible could not be taught in public schools, neither should antibiblical theories. The state's lawyers for the prosecution asserted that those challenging the statute were doing so to advance atheistic views and referred to Darrow's well-known opposition to religion to support their case.

The defense countered that "this theory would absolutely nullify constitutional government and inaugurate the dictatorship of the majority." In oral arguments, defense counsel Arthur Garfield

Hays said that the Fourteenth Amendment to the U.S. Constitution prevented the state from enforcing unreasonable laws and that "Tennessee's 'absurd' antievolution statute violated this standard as much as a law against teaching Copernican astronomy would."[2]

Darrow argued a point that has continued to be invoked to this day: the antievolution statute in question was not designed to foster neutrality in education; rather, opposition to the theory of evolution essentially sprang from a religious foundation that was hostile to science. Thus, any attempt to suppress the teaching of evolution was also effectively an attempt to advance religious views at the expense of science, and this went counter to the purposes of public schools.

Even as the defense made its appeal, they fully expected the Tennessee Supreme Court to rule against them and uphold the lower court conviction, and they set about planning the appeal to the U.S. Supreme Court. There, they hoped to win the case on free speech grounds and thus advance individual liberties.

But through a surprise maneuver, the Tennessee Supreme Court prevented the defense team from achieving its ambition of having the Scopes trial serve as the first major victory for the ACLU in defense of free speech. In its ruling, the court first upheld the constitutionality of the state law, saying that the Butler Act did not give any preference to any religion since it did not require teachers to teach specific subject matter. But it then overturned Scopes's conviction on a technicality that neither side had raised in the appeal or objected to in the original trial: according to Tennessee law, the fine of $100 levied on Scopes should have been set by the jury and not the judge.

Since Scopes was now unexpectedly a man with no conviction against him, no further appeal was possible, and this particular legal battle ended with a whimper instead of a bang, with no constitutional principle established. In fact, the issue of whether it was constitutional to ban the teaching of evolution in public schools was not resolved for another four decades. Following the Scopes trial, opponents of evolution had little success in state legislatures. In the next two years, antievolution bills were proposed but failed in twenty states. The only successes were when the governor of Texas in 1925 banned evolution-related material from textbooks, and in 1926 the Mississippi legislature banned the teaching of evolution in public schools.[3] Then in 1928 Arkansas passed an antievolution statute by popular referendum, and in 1968 this law formed the basis for the first case testing the constitutionality of banning the teaching of evolution to reach the

Every year in the month of July the town of Dayton stages a reenactment of the trial largely based on the actual transcripts. The play was written by Dayton playwright Gale Johnson, and the action takes place in the actual Rhea courthouse courtroom where the original trial was held. Some of the cast members are descendants of actual Scopes trial participants. The basement of the courthouse contains a museum commemorating the trial.

On a hilltop overlooking the town is Bryan College, a Christian college of about seven hundred students founded in 1930 and named after William Jennings Bryan.

U.S. Supreme Court. The Butler Act stayed officially on the Tennessee books, but was not enforced, until 1967, when another biology teacher raised the threat of legal action. The state legislature then decided that having Tennessee associated with one Scopes-like spectacle was enough, and the act was finally repealed.

But while the Scopes trial did not set a major legal precedent, the publicity surrounding it, enhanced by the play and film depicting the trial, has ensured that it has never since been far from the minds of people grappling with the teaching of evolution in schools.

As epilogues to the Scopes case, William Jennings Bryan died in his sleep just five days after the Dayton trial. His death so soon after the grilling by Darrow gave him the air of a martyr and recaptured some of the momentum that the antievolution movement had lost because of the trial. Scopes accepted a scholarship offer to attend the University of Chicago and became a petroleum engineer. For most of the rest of his life, he avoided the limelight and passed up speaking offers, although he did write a memoir many years later. Dayton, Tennessee, returned to being a sleepy little town.

NOTES

1. Edward J. Larson, *Summer for the Gods* (Cambridge, MA: Harvard University Press, 1997), 214.

2. Larson, *Summer for the Gods*, 215.

3. Jeffrey P. Moran, *The Scopes Trial: A Brief History with Documents* (Boston: Bedford/St. Martins, 2002), 216.

Chapter 8

The History of Religion in U.S. Public Schools

To understand the historical context in which the Scopes trial and its aftermath occurred, it is helpful to step back and look at the history of the role of religion in schools in the period that led up to it.

It is interesting to note that at the time of the Scopes trial, religious believers were trying to keep evolution from being taught in the schools because biblical creation theories had already been removed from the curriculum. William Jennings Bryan was essentially arguing for two points: (1) if religion was not to be taught in schools, then neither should evolution, and (2) the community of taxpayers had the right to decide what should be taught in public schools. Bryan contended that the state should be allowed to ban the teaching of evolution since public school teachers were already prohibited from presenting the biblical view of creation.

Bryan's line of argument might puzzle some people today since the common view now is that the banning of religion from public schools is a mid- to late-twentieth-century phenomenon coinciding with the rise of secularism and that, in earlier times, public education was deeply infused with religious teaching.

But the history of religious instruction in U.S. public schools is not so straightforward. In order to understand the real status of religious education in schools leading up to the Scopes trial, we need to go back to the early days of the founding of the republic.

U.S. Supreme Court Justice Felix Frankfurter, in his concurring opinion in the 1948 case *McCollum v. Board of Education*,[1] gives a brief history of the role of religion in schools. (Frankfurter, while at Harvard Law School, also happened to be one of the people who

worked with the ACLU on strategy for the Scopes case.) As Frankfurter pointed out, the original purpose of education was religious
education.

> Traditionally, organized education in the Western world was Church
> education. It could hardly be otherwise when the education of chil-
> dren was primarily study of the Word and the ways of God. Even in
> the Protestant countries, where there was a less close identification of
> Church and State, the basis of education was largely the Bible, and its
> chief purpose inculcation of piety. To the extent that the State inter-
> vened, it used its authority to further aims of the Church.
>
> The emigrants who came to these shores brought this view of educa-
> tion with them. Colonial schools certainly . . . started with a religious
> orientation. When the common problems of the early settlers of the
> Massachusetts Bay Colony revealed the need for common schools, the
> object was the defeat of "one chief project of that old deluder, Satan, to
> keep men from the knowledge of the Scriptures."

But while this broadly religious sentiment was commonly accepted,
the early colonialists and drafters of the Constitution were also
aware, from the history of the countries they had left behind in Europe, that the close identification of government with any particular
religious sect could drive disastrous wedges between people, and
they were uneasy about repeating that history in the United States.

In his opinion in the landmark 1947 case *Everson v. Board of Education*,[2] Justice Hugo Black summarized the abuses that occurred in the
early days of American settlement, which led to the inclusion of the
establishment and free exercise clauses in the First Amendment.

> These practices of the old world were transplanted to, and began to
> thrive in, the soil of the new America. The very charters granted by the
> English Crown to the individuals and companies designated to make
> the laws which would control the destinies of the colonials authorized
> these individuals and companies to erect religious establishments
> which all, whether believers or nonbelievers, would be required to
> support and attend. An exercise of this authority was accompanied
> by a repetition of many of the old-world practices and persecutions.
> Catholics found themselves hounded and proscribed because of their
> faith; Quakers who followed their conscience went to jail; Baptists
> were peculiarly obnoxious to certain dominant Protestant sects; men
> and women of varied faiths who happened to be in a minority in a
> particular locality were persecuted because they steadfastly persisted
> in worshipping God only as their own consciences dictated. And all

of these dissenters were compelled to pay tithes and taxes to support government-sponsored churches whose ministers preached inflammatory sermons designed to strengthen and consolidate the established faith by generating a burning hatred against dissenters.

These practices became so commonplace as to shock the freedom-loving colonials into a feeling of abhorrence. The imposition of taxes to pay ministers' salaries and to build and maintain churches and church property aroused their indignation. It was these feelings which found expression in the First Amendment. No one locality and no one group throughout the Colonies can rightly be given entire credit for having aroused the sentiment that culminated in adoption of the Bill of Rights' provisions embracing religious liberty. But Virginia, where the established church had achieved a dominant influence in political affairs and where many excesses attracted wide public attention, provided a great stimulus and able leadership for the movement. *The people there, as elsewhere, reached the conviction that individual religious liberty could be achieved best under a government which was stripped of all power to tax, to support, or otherwise to assist any or all religions, or to interfere with the beliefs of any religious individual or group.* (My italics)

People were concerned not about the teaching of religious ideas per se, or even about teaching the Bible, but about the influence of any particular religious institution (a "church") in schools. So they tended to oppose any *formal* links between government and religion.

For a flavor of the kind of debate going on at the time, consider James Madison's influential 1785 document called "Memorial and Remonstrance Against Religious Assessments,"[3] which he wrote in opposition to a bill introduced into the General Assembly of Virginia that was designed to levy a tax to support the hiring of teachers of religion in the schools.

In his remonstrance, Madison presciently pointed out that although, at any time, all the people might believe in the same religion and thus feel that there is no problem with the state supporting it, once state support of religion was allowed, it would not take much for narrower and narrower sectarian interests to jockey for control to give particular beliefs pride of place at the expense of others. He said,

> Who does not see that the same authority which can establish Christianity, in exclusion of all other Religions, may establish with the same ease any particular sect of Christians, in exclusion of all other Sects? that the same authority which can force a citizen to contribute three

pence only of his property for the support of any one establishment, may force him to conform to any other establishment in all cases whatsoever? . . .

Whilst we assert for ourselves a freedom to embrace, to profess and to observe the Religion which we believe to be of divine origin, we cannot deny an equal freedom to those whose minds have not yet yielded to the evidence which has convinced us. . . .

Experience witnesseth that ecclesiastical establishments, instead of maintaining the purity and efficacy of Religion, have had a contrary operation. During almost fifteen centuries has the legal establishment of Christianity been on trial. What have been its fruits? More or less in all places, pride and indolence in the Clergy, ignorance and servility in the laity, in both, superstition, bigotry and persecution.

Partly because of Madison's powerful arguments against state support of religion, the bill did not pass; instead, the Virginia legislature in 1786 enacted Thomas Jefferson's Bill for Religious Freedom,[4] which actually reversed the process and disestablished the official church of that state.

So, at the close of the eighteenth century, Americans, even though they were broadly religious, saw the dangers of a close identification of a church with the state and were thus wary of any formal entanglement of the government with any specific sect or church.

But while explicit support for specific religious instruction to advance a particular sectarian view was frowned upon, the fact that almost all the colonialists were Protestants meant that they saw much of what we would now view as religious education simply as ordinary education. Their view of the purpose of schooling was closely tied with teaching morals and values, and these were believed to be religiously based. So, while people were cool to the idea of the state supporting specific churches, they did not view a generic Protestant Christian ideology as representing a "church." Rather, they perceived it merely as the set of personal beliefs that most people just happened to share and thus as "natural."

Since schools were under local control, and hence represent relatively homogeneous groups of Protestants, no challenges emerged to such tacit support for a generic Protestant religious ideology in those communities. As Philip Hamburger writes in *Separation of Church and State*, even in New York City, which was more diverse than the rest of the nation, the idea of a generic Protestantism as being merely neutral and not explicitly religious held sway.

Since the early 1820s, when it first acquired authority to distribute public school funds, New York's City Council had denied such funds to all sectarian institutions, including Baptist, Methodist, and Catholic schools. Instead, it gave most of its funds to the schools run by the Public School Society—a privately operated nondenominational organization. Yet the ostensibly nonsectarian schools of the Public School Society had some broadly Protestant, if not narrowly sectarian, characteristics. One goal of the society was "to inculcate the sublime truths of religion and morality contained in the Holy Scriptures," and its schools required children to read the King James Bible and to use textbooks in which Catholics were condemned as deceitful, bigoted, and intolerant.[5]

Not surprisingly, Catholics did not share the view that this was a religiously neutral education, and as the number of Catholics in the city rose due to immigration from Ireland, they started pressing for public funds to create their own schools free of anti-Catholic bias and to teach their own brand of Christianity.

But Catholics were widely seen at that time as being too monolithic a body, as too subservient in their thinking to their priests and the pope, and thus their allegiance to the new republic was considered suspect. Some non-Catholics even went to the extent of suggesting that since the Catholic Church seemed to demand great obedience from its parishioners, such people had ceased to be independent thinkers and were thus not even worthy of being allowed to vote in a democracy.[6]

When Catholics pointed out that the Public School Society could hardly claim to be religiously neutral since it required students to read the King James Bible and other religious materials, that body "defended its position that its publicly supported schools were nonsectarian by offering to black out the most bigoted anti-Catholic references in the textbooks. It refused, however, to withdraw the King James Bible, which, although Protestant, no longer seemed to belong to any church."[7]

Catholics' request for funding for their own schools was opposed because it seemed to lead to an alliance of church and state. In fact, it was to deny these Catholic demands that the stronger idea of *separation* of church and state gained popularity. Up to that point, people had largely viewed the founding principles of the country, as enshrined in its constitution and associated documents, as *prohibiting a union* of the state with an organized church.

In 1802, Thomas Jefferson, then president of the United States, raised the idea of the separation of church and state in a famous letter to a committee of the Danbury Baptist Association, in which he wrote, "I contemplate with sovereign reverence that act of the whole American people which declared that *their* legislature should 'make no law respecting an establishment of religion, or prohibiting the free exercise thereof,' thus building a wall of separation between Church & State."[8]

Some have argued that because Jefferson endorsed the "wall of separation"—this was the first time he introduced that powerful and influential metaphor—in a letter and not some major public pronouncement, it should not be given much weight. But the history and context that prompted the letter suggest that it was not part of a casual correspondence but that Jefferson was deliberately using it as an opportunity to make a statement about the proper role for religion in a democratic society.[9]

Jefferson's view (advocating a separation of church and state) was much stronger than the existing one (preventing a union of church and state), and it started gaining ground in the mid-nineteenth century onwards, mainly as an argument to prevent Catholics from gaining funding for their own denominational schools.

This idea of separation gained further ground when Pope Gregory XVI, in an encyclical published in 1832, condemned the doctrine of separation of church and state, presumably because he suspected that its underlying purpose was to argue against public funding of Catholic schools. This move backfired because the intervention of a pope in the internal politics of the country increased the fears of Protestants in America that the Catholics sought to dominate the United States; thus, it increased support for the doctrine of separation of church and state as a way of limiting Catholics' ambitions.

As I said before, the various Protestant sects could embrace this separation doctrine because they did not see themselves as acting as a single "church" but as individuals who happened to share a broad Protestant religious ethic. They thus excluded themselves from the "sectarian" label and saw the separation of church and state as a way of maintaining the status quo in which a generic Protestant ideology was pervasive.

Like so many other Protestants, Baptists desired to exclude any particular church from public institutions but welcomed Bible reading and other elements of Protestant religion, which seemed to be the faith of free individuals. In the 1870s, for example, although some Baptists protested the introduction of the Bible into public schools and argued that "the state had no right to teach religion," most Baptists saw no reason to go so far. As one Baptist, George C. Lorimer, explained in 1877: "The position of the Bible in the schools is not the result of any union between Protestants and the State; nor was it secured by the political action of one denomination, or of all combined. The Church, as such, did not put it there, and the Church, as such, cannot take it away. Instead, the 'people' put the Bible in the schools."[10]

So, even as the idea of the separation of church and state was gaining popularity, it was not initially seen as a call for the separation of Christianity and the state. When a belief structure is ubiquitous, its adherents (in this case Protestant Christians) tend to see it as "normal," "natural," and "obviously true," not as merely one of a spectrum of possible views.

As the idea of separation of church and state became more widely accepted, it was inevitable that some people, especially those who did not share these common religious beliefs, would see the benefits of extending that concept to mean that there should be a complete separation of *religion* (including Protestant Christianity) and the state. Initial calls for this stronger separation took the form of arguing that this was what the Founding Fathers had desired but not explicitly provided for in the Constitution. Thus, there began to be calls for a constitutional amendment to more firmly entrench this principle in the rule of law.

These calls for a constitutional amendment mandating the separation of church and state gained ground. As part of this drive, there were calls to remove chaplains from publicly supported institutions, prohibit the use of the Bible (either as a textbook or as a source of religious worship) in public schools, replace religious judicial oaths with secular affirmations, abolish tax exemptions for religious institutions, and so on.[11] Even President Ulysses S. Grant urged stronger separation when he said in his 1875 State of the Union address that the United States should "declare Church and State forever separate and distinct, but each free within their proper spheres."[12]

In an 1875 speech to the Convention of the Army of the Tennessee, Grant said that the country should "encourage free schools and resolve that not one dollar appropriated for their support shall be appropriated for the support of any sectarian schools. Resolve that neither the State nor the nation, nor both combined, shall support institutions of learning other than those sufficient to afford every child growing up in the land the opportunity of a good common school education, unmixed with sectarian, pagan, or atheistical dogmas. Leave the matter of religion to the family altar, the church, and the private school, supported entirely by private contributions. Keep the Church and State forever separated."[13]

The idea of an amendment to the U.S. Constitution implementing stronger separation reached its peak around 1875 but failed to come to fruition, and that plan was eventually abandoned. But it did achieve some results, with Congress passing laws requiring any *new* state seeking admittance to the union to have clauses in its state constitution mandating the separation of church and state.

Following their failure to have the separation of church and state incorporated into the U.S. Constitution, proponents of separation in the late nineteenth century then shifted strategy, urging changes in state constitutions and arguing that the federal constitution had *implicitly* advocated separation all along and that what was necessary was a *reinterpretation* of its key clauses to more clearly reflect that understanding.

A broad coalition of forces—which included Baptists, Jews, atheists, Masons, and the Ku Klux Klan—supported this idea, some to prevent the encroachment into government by particular religious sects (especially Catholics), others because they really did want *all* religion out of government institutions.[14] Thus, the *idea* of the separation of church and state, although not explicitly stated in the federal constitution, became widely accepted as a basic underlying principle of the country.

Because the idea of separation had gained considerable popularity by the time of World War I, state supreme courts in several states had started questioning the practice of Bible reading in public schools.[15] Use of the Bible in public schools started decreasing to such an extent that parents started becoming concerned that the pendulum had swung too far, that the public schools were providing too little or no religious instruction at all.

A Baptist minister in 1919 put it this way: the tendency "toward the complete secularization of education . . . had grown out of an overemphasis of our doctrine of separation of religious freedom." He felt that Baptists "have been so insistent on the separation of church and state that we have almost completely separated education and religion to the serious detriment of both."[16] Another Baptist summarized how this situation had come to pass:

> Two forces, from opposite sides, have cooperated towards this general secularizing of our education. . . . First, the Christian forces insisted on the absolute separation of Church and State, and thought of all religion in terms of church creeds and forms. Hence they set themselves against the teaching of Christianity in schools supported by public funds and controlled by boards of education. At the same time non-Christian influences were exerted by men who, like the churchmen, identified religion with the creeds of organized churches and felt that the churches would produce friction and confusion in the schools, would lay a hindering hand on freedom of thought and investigation. Thus the two operated together to eliminate religion from our education.[17]

This was the climate in which the Scopes trial took place in 1925, which explains the line of argument William Jennings Bryan pursued. It was a time when teaching of the Bible had largely disappeared from schools as a matter of formal educational policy. The religious practices that still remained tended to be local, small in scale, and idiosyncratic.

Rather than directly challenging the by then accepted idea of separation of church and state and attempting to reverse the secularizing trends that had removed the Bible from formal public school education, Bryan instead tried to use the separation idea to his advantage, arguing that evolution was not a scientific fact but merely an idea based on an atheist doctrine akin to a religion and thus violated the "wall of separation" just as surely as Bible instruction did.

This line of argument, that the theory of evolution is less a scientific theory than an atheist-inspired belief structure, is still widely propagated today by evolution's opponents.

NOTES

1. *McCollum v. Board of Education*, 333 U.S. 203, www.law.cornell.edu/supct/html/historics/USSC_CR_0333_0203_ZO.html.

2. *Everson v. Board of Education*, 330 U.S. 1, www.law.cornell.edu/supct/html/historics/USSC_CR_0330_0001_ZO.html.

3. See religiousfreedom.lib.virginia.edu/sacred/madison_m&r_1785.html.

4. See www.churchstatelaw.com/historicalmaterials/8_1_3_2.asp.

5. Philip Hamburger, *Separation of Church and State* (Cambridge, MA: Harvard University Press, 2002), 220. It has been suggested that Hamburger lays too much emphasis on the role that anti-Catholic bias played in the church-state separation movement. For other perspectives, see Isaac Kramnick and R. Laurence Moore, *The Godless Constitution: The Case Against Religious Correctness* (New York: W. W. Norton & Company, 1996) and Leonard W. Levy, *The Establishment Clause: Religion and the First Amendment* (Chapel Hill, The University of North Carolina, 1994).

6. Hamburger, *Separation of Church and State*, 234–46.

7. Hamburger, *Separation of Church and State*, 223.

8. Hamburger, *Separation of Church and State*, 1.

9. Rob Boston, "Priority Mail: Why President Jefferson's Letter to the Danbury Baptists Is Still Being Read by Americans after 200 Years," Americans United, January 2002, www.au.org/site/News2?abbr=cs_&page=NewsArticle&id=5609&security=1001&news_iv_ctrl=1046.

10. Hamburger, *Separation of Church and State*, 283–84.

11. Hamburger, *Separation of Church and State*, 302–4.

12. Hamburger, *Separation of Church and State*, 323.

13. Hamburger, *Separation of Church and State*, 322.

14. Hamburger, *Separation of Church and State*, 481.

15. Hamburger, *Separation of Church and State*, 369.

16. Hamburger, *Separation of Church and State*, 383.

17. Hamburger, *Separation of Church and State*, 383.

Chapter 9

Religion and the Establishment Clause after *Scopes*

As the debate over evolution and religion continued after the Scopes trial ended, subsequent court cases can best be understood as being brought by those who felt that separation of *church* and state had been interpreted too broadly to mean the separation of *religion* and state. They wanted to put at least some religion back into schools.

To understand legal developments after *Scopes*, recall that prior to 1925, the First Amendment was seen to apply restrictions only on the powers of the *federal* government. It was the 1925 *Gitlow v. New York* case that expanded the free speech and free press protections from infringement by state and local governments as well by incorporating them under the Fourteenth Amendment.

Then, in 1940, in the case *Cantwell v. Connecticut*,[1] the right of Jehovah's Witnesses to spread their message on a public street without seeking prior government approval was upheld unanimously by the U.S. Supreme Court, with the Court agreeing with the Jehovah's Witnesses that such restrictions violated the First Amendment's free exercise of religion clause and that this clause was also explicitly applicable to the states under the Fourteenth Amendment.

In *Cantwell*, the Court stated even more expansively, "The fundamental concept of liberty embodied in that Amendment embraces the liberties guaranteed by the First Amendment. . . . The First Amendment declares that Congress shall make no law respecting an establishment of religion or prohibiting the free exercise thereof. The Fourteenth Amendment has rendered the legislatures of the states as incompetent as Congress to enact such laws."

A key development centered on whether the Establishment Clause was also binding on the states. Although the Supreme Court had stated that it was in the Cantwell case, only the free exercise clause had really been at issue there. The case that definitively settled the Establishment Clause issue was 1947's *Everson v. Board of Education*.[2]

Everson involved a challenge to the policy of a local school district in New Jersey to reimburse parents for the cost of bus transportation for their children to attend parochial schools. In a close 5–4 decision, the Court ruled that doing so did *not* violate the idea of separation of church and state. The majority ruled that such actions fell into the category of maintaining citizens' general welfare and that carrying the idea of separation to such extremes so that no interaction at all could exist between the state and parochial schools might prevent the state from providing even police or fire or other minimal protections and services to those schools.

Writing for the majority, Justice Hugo Black said,

> Measured by these standards, we cannot say that the First Amendment prohibits New Jersey from spending tax-raised funds to pay the bus fares of parochial school pupils as a part of a general program under which it pays the fares of pupils attending public and other schools. . . .
>
> Moreover, state-paid policemen, detailed to protect children going to and from church schools from the very real hazards of traffic, would serve much the same purpose and accomplish much the same result as state provisions intended to guarantee free transportation of a kind which the state deems to be best for the school children's welfare. . . .
>
> Of course, cutting off church schools from these services so separate and so indisputably marked off from the religious function would make it far more difficult for the schools to operate. But such is obviously not the purpose of the First Amendment. That Amendment *requires the state to be a neutral in its relations with groups of religious believers and nonbelievers*; it does not require the state to be their adversary. State power is no more to be used so as to handicap religions than it is to favor them. (My italics)

The Establishment Clause

Congress shall make no law respecting an establishment of religion.

At first, this ruling was seen as a major constitutional defeat for the principle of separation of church and state, and Black, the author of the majority verdict, came in for severe criticism. Black has played an important role in the development of judicial doctrine on church-state relations, and his profound influence on the interpretation of the Establishment Clause, as well as his own personal history, is interesting enough to justify a digression about him.

Black had once been a member of the Ku Klux Klan (KKK) in his native Alabama, although he did not acknowledge his membership until after his appointment to the Supreme Court. Before his 1937 elevation to the Supreme Court by Franklin Delano Roosevelt, Black had been elected to the U.S. Senate from Alabama in 1926 with strong support from the KKK and other groups that strongly supported the idea of church-state separation and thought he would strengthen that position. Conversely, his nomination to the Supreme Court had been especially criticized by Catholics, who saw him as opposed to them.

His ruling in *Everson* was seen as a sop to Catholics, an attempt to deflect charges of being anti-Catholic, and thus viewed as a letdown by those supporters who had rallied to his defense against the Catholics.

But although advocates of church-state separation criticized his *Everson* ruling, it actually laid the foundations for subsequent rulings that more firmly established the idea that religion and the state should stay separate because of its explicit assertion that the Establishment Clause protections of the First Amendment were also binding on state and local governments by virtue of the Fourteenth Amendment.

Justice Black said, "The broad meaning given the [First] Amendment by these earlier cases has been accepted by this Court in its decisions concerning an individual's religious freedom rendered since the Fourteenth Amendment was interpreted to make the prohibitions of the First applicable to state action abridging religious freedom. There is every reason to give the same application and broad interpretation to the 'establishment of religion' clause."

(Today all the provisions of the First Amendment have been ruled to apply to the states, and the Supreme Court has also long held that local governments are subject to the same constitutional limitations as the states because local governments are legally regarded as units of the states.)

Even more importantly, *Everson* also set general guidelines for what the Establishment Clause should be taken to mean, and Thomas Jefferson's "wall of separation between church and state" was explicitly inserted into the ruling, making that famous phrase part of constitutional law for the first time. Writing for the Court, Justice Black penned what has since become a major part of the framework for interpreting the Establishment Clause:

> The "establishment of religion" clause of the First Amendment means at least this: Neither a state nor the Federal Government can set up a church. Neither can pass laws which aid one religion, aid all religions, or prefer one religion over another. Neither can force nor influence a person to go to or to remain away from church against his will or force him to profess a belief or disbelief in any religion. No person can be punished for entertaining or professing religious beliefs or disbeliefs, for church-attendance or non-attendance. No tax, large or small, can be levied to support any religious activities or institutions, whatever they may be called, or whatever form they may adopt to teach or prac- tice religion. Neither a state nor the Federal Government can, openly or secretly, participate in the affairs of any religious organizations or groups and vice versa. In the words of Jefferson, the clause . . . was intended to erect "a wall of separation between church and State."

As Edward J. Larson points out in *Summer for the Gods*,[3] after *Everson*, "the Court quickly began purging well-entrenched reli- gious practices and influences from state-supported schools." The precedent set in this case rapidly led to a whole series of Supreme Court decisions, several of whose opinions were authored by Black, creating greater distance between religion and state and especially removing religion from schools.

Philip Hamburger suggests[4] that Black was well aware that this would happen and that his *Everson* ruling, which seemingly favored the interests of parochial Catholic schools, was a shrewd move on his part, giving a small victory to parochial schools and thus mollifying those critics who suspected him of anti-Catholic bias because of his KKK past, while at the same time laying the foundation for advancing the larger idea of separation of church and state, which he strongly supported but which Catholics felt was aimed at restricting them.

Thus, by the first half of the twentieth century, the idea of the separation of church and state had taken such hold in the country that most formal religion-based practices had been taken out of the schools. As religious groups tried to get more religion back into the schools, their efforts led to more court cases.

The next major religion in schools case came in 1948, the year following the landmark *Everson* ruling. In *McCollum v. Board of Education*,[5] religious instruction in public schools was first *explicitly* ruled to be unconstitutional under the U.S. Constitution.

This case involved a challenge to the growing practice of public schools granting "release time" for the teaching of religion. This practice arose because some parents felt that relegating religious instruction to just the weekends, to be performed by private individuals or priests, diminished the importance of religion in the eyes of children when compared to the secular curriculum taught as part of the regular school day. So they requested and received permission from schools to use part of the school day to teach religion, although the details of implementation varied from place to place.

A local public school in Illinois established a policy whereby thirty to forty-five minutes were set aside each week for teachers of religion, paid by a private consortium of religious organizations, to come to the schools to provide religious instruction to students whose parents had consented to have them attend. Children of parents who did not want such instruction had to leave their classrooms and go to other parts of the building for secular studies. One such parent challenged the practice, and the case went all the way to the U.S. Supreme Court.

The Supreme Court in an 8–1 decision ruled that this practice was unconstitutional and effectively barred *all* religious instruction within public schools. Citing the *Everson* guidelines, Justice Black in his majority opinion struck down such "release-time" policies involving the use of public school buildings and time to further religious education. He again emphasized the importance of strengthening the separation of church and state:

> [The policy] is beyond all question a utilization of the tax-established and tax-supported public school system to aid religious groups to spread their faith. . . .
>
> For the First Amendment rests upon the premise that both religion and government can best work to achieve their lofty aims if each is left free from the other within its respective sphere. Or, as we said in the Everson case, the First Amendment has erected a wall between Church and State which must be kept high and impregnable.

Here not only are the State's tax-supported public school buildings used for the dissemination of religious doctrines. The State also affords sectarian groups an invaluable aid in that it helps to provide pupils for their religious classes through use of the State's compulsory public school machinery. This is not separation of Church and State.

The year 1952 saw a variant of the McCollum case. In *Zorach v. Clauson*,[6] a challenge was brought against a policy in which schools authorized students, on the written request of their parents, *to leave the school buildings and grounds during school hours* to go to religious centers for religious instruction or devotional exercises. In this case, the U.S. Supreme Court ruled in a split decision that this practice did *not* violate the Establishment Clause.

The next major case that resulted in further separation of religion and schools was 1962's *Engel v. Vitale.*[7] The New York State Board of Regents had adopted a policy whereby each class had to begin each day by saying aloud in the presence of the teacher the following prayer: "Almighty God, we acknowledge our dependence upon Thee, and we beg Thy blessings upon us, our parents, our teachers and our Country."

Ten parents filed an objection to this so-called Regents' prayer. The U.S. Supreme Court struck down the policy, saying that such governmentally composed prayers, even if every student were not compelled to say them aloud, were unconstitutional. The ruling said that "state officials may not compose an official state prayer and require that it be recited in the public schools of the State at the beginning of each school day—even if the prayer is denominationally neutral and pupils who wish to do so may remain silent or be excused from the room while the prayer is being recited."

Justice Black was again the author of this 6–1 majority opinion, in which he said,

> The respondents' argument to the contrary, which is largely based upon the contention that the Regents' prayer is "nondenominational" and the fact that the program, as modified and approved by state courts, does not require all pupils to recite the prayer, but permits those who wish to do so to remain silent or be excused from the room, ignores the essential nature of the program's constitutional defects. . . . *When the power, prestige and financial support of government is placed behind a particular religious belief, the indirect coercive pressure upon religious minorities to conform to the prevailing officially approved religion is plain.* (My italics)

He drew upon history, arguing that the early colonialists had tried to escape precisely this kind of state-sponsored religious practice in Europe, and he deplored the tendency of people who oppose certain acts when they are in the minority to reverse course abruptly when they become the majority. "It is a matter of history that this very practice of establishing governmentally composed prayers for religious services was one of the reasons which caused many of our early colonists to leave England and seek religious freedom in America. . . . It is an unfortunate fact of history that, when some of the very groups which had most strenuously opposed the established Church of England found themselves sufficiently in control of colonial governments in this country to write their own prayers into law, they passed laws making their own religion the official religion of their respective colonies."

Black rejected the argument that prohibiting such practices demonstrated hostility to religion. He said that the Founding Fathers were instead trying to avoid the pitfalls that inevitably ensue when religion and the state get entangled, adding that they had "well justified fears which nearly all of them felt arising out of an awareness that governments of the past had shackled men's tongues to make them speak only the religious thoughts that government wanted them to speak and to pray only to the God that government wanted them to pray to."

Although the Supreme Court in *Engel* ruled that having students say a state-drafted "official" prayer, however generic, was an unconstitutional violation of the Establishment Clause, it left open the constitutionality of "spontaneous" prayers not written by the state. Soon after, in 1963, *School District of Abington Township, Pennsylvania v. Schempp*[8] addressed this very issue.

This Supreme Court case actually dealt with two cases taken together. In one (*Abington v. Schempp*), the state of Pennsylvania had passed a law saying, "At least ten verses from the Holy Bible shall be read, without comment, at the opening of each public school on each school day. Any child shall be excused from such Bible reading, or attending such Bible reading, upon the written request of his parent or guardian."

The companion case (*Murray v. Curlett*) received a lot more publicity because it was brought by the prominent atheist Madalyn Murray (later Madalyn Murray O'Hair). This case involved a challenge to a 1905 Maryland law that required starting the school day with a reading, without comment, of a passage from the Bible and/or saying the Lord's Prayer. Parents who objected to the practice could, however, request that their children be excused from this exercise.

The U.S. Supreme Court overturned both policies, ruling that "no state law or school board may require that passages from the Bible be read or that the Lord's Prayer be recited in the public schools of a State at the beginning of each school day."

In writing the majority opinion (which included Justice Black), Justice Thomas Clark dismissed the claim that keeping religion out of schools was equivalent to fostering another religion, that of "secularism." William Jennings Bryan had made this argument at the time of the Scopes trial, and one still hears it today. Justice Clark wrote,

It is insisted that, unless these religious exercises are permitted, a "religion of secularism" is established in the schools. We agree, of course, that the State may not establish a "religion of secularism" in the sense of *affirmatively* opposing or showing hostility to religion, thus "preferring those who believe in no religion over those who do believe." We do not agree, however, that this decision in any sense has that effect. In addition, it might well be said that one's education is not complete without a study of comparative religion or the history of religion and its relationship to the advancement of civilization. It certainly may be said that the Bible is worthy of study for its literary and historic qualities. Nothing we have said here indicates that such study of the Bible or of religion, *when presented objectively as part of a secular program of education*, may not be effected consistently with the First Amendment. But the exercises here do not fall into those categories. They are religious exercises, required by the States in violation of the command of the First Amendment that the Government maintain strict neutrality, neither aiding nor opposing religion. (My italics)

All these cases set the stage for the first test, four decades after *Scopes*, of the constitutionality of banning the teaching of evolution in public schools.

NOTES

1. *Cantwell v. Connecticut*, 310 U.S. 296, www.law.cornell.edu/supct/html/historics/USSC_CR_0310_0296_ZO.html.

2. *Everson v. Board of Education*, 330 U.S. 1, www.law.cornell.edu/supct/html/historics/USSC_CR_0330_0001_ZO.html.

3. Edward J. Larson, *Summer for the Gods* (Cambridge, MA: Harvard University Press, 1997), 249.

4. Philip Hamburger, *Separation of Church and State* (Cambridge, MA: Harvard University Press, 2002), 462.

5. *McCollum v. Board of Education*, 333 U.S. 203, www.law.cornell.edu/supct/html/historics/USSC_CR_0333_0203_ZO.html.

6. *Zorach v. Clauson*, 343 U.S. 306, www.law.cornell.edu/supct/html/historics/USSC_CR_0343_0306_ZO.html.

7. *Engel v. Vitale*, 370 U.S. 421, www.law.cornell.edu/supct/html/historics/USSC_CR_0370_0421_ZO.html.

8. *School District of Abington Township, Pennsylvania v. Schempp*, 374 U.S. 203, www.law.cornell.edu/supct/html/historics/USSC_CR_0374_0203_ZO.html.

Chapter 10

Evolution Back in the Courts

In the forty years that had passed since the Scopes trial in 1925, opposition to the teaching of evolution had remained strong, and antievolution laws, such as Tennessee's Butler Act, still remained on the books, though they were not enforced, possibly because of the negative publicity generated by the Scopes trial. But that period of dormancy was soon to end.

The mid-1960s saw the reemergence of controversies over the teaching of evolution, and three states (Tennessee, Arkansas, and Louisiana) played central roles in the renewed legislative efforts to combat the teaching of evolution in public schools.

> Popular support for teaching a Bible-based creation model was by no means eliminated by the adverse publicity generated by the Scopes case, and the 1960s saw a dramatic resurgence in creationist views, as well as a shift in their emphasis. Ironically . . . this newer version, now bearing the name of "creation science," was even less accommodating of mainstream scientific views than the creationist views advocated by William Jennings Bryan during the Scopes trial. As creation science gained popularity, it was accompanied by attempts to displace evolutionary theory from its dominant position within the educational system as *the* explanation for the origin of life. The main arenas for these battles were local school districts, and primarily involved the selection of textbooks. Textbook publishers, wary of losing lucrative markets, were under increasing pressure to either eliminate Darwinian evolution theory entirely from textbooks or to tone down its claims to success and offer alternative, implicitly creationist, versions as well. It was inevitable that the conflict would sooner or later spill over in the legal arena.[1]

The 1961 publication of John Whitcomb and Henry M. Morris's *The Genesis Flood* facilitated the rise of the creationist movement.[2] This book tried to make the case that *scientific* evidence supported a strictly literal interpretation of the Bible, down to a six-thousand-year-old Earth and Noah's flood. While Whitcomb was a theologian, Morris had a doctoral degree in hydraulic engineering with minors in geology and mathematics. He later founded the Institute for Creation Research in 1970 to advance these ideas.

These new creationist groups took the Bible even more literally than William Jennings Bryan; in fact, they thought that Bryan had betrayed Christianity during the Scopes trial by allowing that the creation days of Genesis may have lasted longer than twenty-four hours, thus allowing for the possibility that the universe had been around for more than six thousand years.

The new creationists were having none of that wishy-washiness. Coupled with their strict literal interpretation of the Bible was the powerful feeling that the teaching of evolution had to be countered.

Initial challenges to the theory of evolution took the form of demands that schools and textbook publishers acknowledge that Darwinian evolution was "only a theory," not a scientific "fact," and hence should be eliminated from the science curriculum since science was supposed to be only concerned with facts.

But these initial challenges had only minor success. Schools and teachers could hardly be expected not to say anything at all to students about how life and the universe came to be. Since Darwinian evolution had become accepted by professional scientists as the main organizing principle in understanding the appearance of different life forms, it was inevitable that science textbooks and the training of science teachers would reflect that thinking, albeit in a fairly ad-hoc manner.

The paradox was that despite the near universal teaching (in one form or another) of Darwinian evolution in schools, surveys showed a surprising resistance among the general public to key tenets of the theory, especially the one that said that humans and apes had common ancestors. As recently as 1988, 38% of college students believed that human life originated in the Garden of Eden. Feeling that perhaps the reason for this state of affairs was that evolution was not being taught properly, the scientific community planned and implemented a thoroughgoing reform of biology science texts, culminating in the 1960s with the BSCS (Biological Sciences Curriculum Study) textbook series that had evolutionary ideas as a major theme permeating the texts. In these books, there was no escaping the fact that evolution was seen as *the* organizing principle in biology with no viable alternative.

The BSCS series was widely adopted by schools; but was perceived by creationists as a direct assault by the scientific community on their religious beliefs and galvanized them into responding.[3]

Part of the impetus for better science education was the shock created by the 1957 launch of the Sputnik satellite. The sense of panic that accompanied the idea that the United States was falling behind the Soviet Union in science and technology and thus might lose the Cold War no doubt helped policy makers override the sentiments of religious believers. But the fact that some laws against the teaching of evolution were still on the books meant that the issue was far from settled.

In 1928, Arkansas had passed a law similar to Tennessee's 1925 Butler Act, prohibiting any mention of evolution in state-approved textbooks. Not until 1968 did the question of whether schools could ban the teaching of evolution finally reach the U.S. Supreme Court, triggered by the 1928 Arkansas law. Although none of the Supreme Court decisions to that point had dealt directly with the teaching of evolution, and thus there was no legal precedent dealing specifically with that particular topic, all the other Establishment Clause cases set the stage on which the constitutional issues relating to the teaching of evolution would be adjudicated.

The Arkansas law in question had been passed by popular referendum and made it unlawful for a teacher in any state-supported school or university to teach or to use a textbook that taught "that mankind ascended or descended from a lower order of animals." This law, like the Butler Act after *Scopes*, was never enforced.

In 1965, however, Arkansas adopted the BSCS textbooks that emphasized evolution, and since the 1928 law was still on the books, and since the new textbooks explicitly required the teaching of evolution, any biology teacher was potentially subject to a charge of violating the law. The state teachers' organization saw the opportunity to put the law to the test and challenged it using, as in *Scopes*, another young biology teacher (Susan Epperson) as the key player, this time as the lead plaintiff challenging the validity of the law rather than as someone accused of breaking it.

(As an aside, while the Arkansas case worked its way through the legal system, in Tennessee another teacher, Gary Scott, was threatening to take similar legal action against the Butler Act. This case was initiated in 1967 and, coming along at the same time as the release of the memoirs of John Scopes, had the potential to make Tennessee the laughing stock of the nation again. This put pressure on the state legislature, which finally decided in that same year to repeal the Butler Act, bringing that particular chapter of the religion-evolution wars to a close.)

In the case of *Epperson v. Arkansas*,[4] the trial judge ruled in favor of Epperson and overturned the law on the grounds that it unconstitutionally limited the teacher's freedom to teach about theories of origins. The state appealed, and the Arkansas Supreme Court overruled the trial judge, saying that the Arkansas law was a valid exercise of the state's power to specify the curriculum in public schools. Epperson then took the challenge to the U.S. Supreme Court.

So, after the passage of more than four decades, the issue that had riveted the nation when Clarence Darrow and William Jennings Bryan argued the point in Tennessee in 1925 finally reached the highest legal levels. The Epperson case achieved what the Scopes case had aspired to do but failed: it became an evolution-based First Amendment test case to be adjudicated by the U.S. Supreme Court.

In 1968 in *Epperson v. Arkansas*, the U.S. Supreme Court ruled *unanimously* that the statute effectively banning the teaching of evolution was unconstitutional.

But while the Court was emphatic in its decision, its member justices did not agree on the reasoning behind it. Most initially wanted to overturn the statute on the grounds that it was too vague rather than that it violated the Establishment Clause; in the end, however, Justice Abe Fortas persuaded the majority to rule that it was indeed a violation of the First Amendment Establishment Clause. In his majority *Epperson* ruling, Justice Fortas said,

> The overriding fact is that Arkansas' law selects from the body of knowledge a particular segment which it proscribes for the sole reason that it is deemed to conflict with a particular religious doctrine; that is, with a particular interpretation of the Book of Genesis by a particular religious group. . . .
>
> The First Amendment mandates governmental neutrality between religion and religion, and between religion and nonreligion. . . .
>
> *The State's undoubted right to prescribe the curriculum for its public schools does not carry with it the right to prohibit, on pain of criminal penalty,*

the teaching of a scientific theory or doctrine where that prohibition is based
upon reasons that violate the First Amendment. . . .
    Arkansas' law cannot be defended as an act of religious neutrality.
Arkansas did not seek to excise from the curricula of its schools and
universities all discussion of the origin of man. The law's effort was
confined to an attempt to blot out a particular theory because of its
supposed conflict with the Biblical account, literally read. (My italics)

Note that in the italicized section, the Court rejects simple majoritarian thinking, saying that constitutional restrictions do limit the
power of school boards to completely prescribe the curriculum.

While the 1968 *Epperson* ruling was a clear victory for the teaching
of evolution and provided the definitive answer that the Scopes case
had sought and failed to deliver, the opinions of the various justices
provide some perspectives and arguments that are worth reviewing.

One interesting feature of the ruling was how the shadow of
Scopes influenced the justices' thinking. In fact, Fortas resurrected
the ghost of the Scopes trial in his opinion, referring to the "sensational publicity" surrounding it.

Another notable feature was how, although the verdict was
unanimous, the reasoning by the various justices influenced the
strategies adopted in later attempts to combat the teaching of evolution. In stating their different reasons for overturning the statute,
Justices Abe Fortas and Hugo Black echoed some of the arguments
used nearly a half century earlier by Clarence Darrow and William
Jennings Bryan.

In his majority opinion, Fortas took roughly the Darrow position,
saying, "While study of religions and of the Bible from a literary
and historic viewpoint, presented objectively as part of a secular
program of education, need not collide with the First Amendment's

---

First Amendment

Congress shall make no law respecting an establishment of
religion, or prohibiting the free exercise thereof; or abridging the freedom of speech, or of the press; or the right
of the people peaceably to assemble, and to petition the
Government for a redress of grievances.

prohibition, the State may not adopt programs or practices in its public schools or colleges which 'aid or oppose' any religion. This prohibition is absolute. It forbids alike the preference of a religious doctrine or *the prohibition of theory which is deemed antagonistic to a particular dogma"* (my italics).

Black, however, was uneasy about the reach of the ruling on Establishment Clause grounds, preferring to rule it unconstitutional because of its *vagueness,* on the basis of the Fourteenth Amendment's "due process" clause, saying,[5] "Under this statute, as construed by the Arkansas Supreme Court, a teacher cannot know whether he is forbidden to mention Darwin's theory at all or only free to discuss it as long as he refrains from contending that it is true. It is an established rule that a statute which leaves an ordinary man so doubtful about its meaning that he cannot know when he has violated it denies him the first essential of due process."

Black seemed sympathetic to Bryan's point that the people's right (expressed through the agencies of government) to determine what should be taught in schools should not be dismissed too easily.

> It may be, instead, that the people's motive was merely that it would be best to remove this controversial subject from its schools; there is no reason I can imagine why a State is without power to withdraw from its curriculum any subject deemed too emotional and controversial for its public schools. And this Court has consistently held that it is not for us to invalidate a statute because of our views that the "motives" behind its passage were improper; it is simply too difficult to determine what those motives were. . . .
>
> I am also not ready to hold that a person hired to teach school children takes with him into the classroom a constitutional right to teach sociological, economic, political, or religious subjects that the school's managers do not want discussed. This Court has said that the rights of free speech, "while fundamental in our democratic society, still do not mean that everyone with opinions or beliefs to express may address a group at any public place and at any time." . . .
>
> I question whether it is absolutely certain, as the Court's opinion indicates, that "academic freedom" permits a teacher to breach his contractual agreement to teach only the subjects designated by the school authorities who hired him.

Justice Potter Stewart concurred with Black, agreeing that the statute was unconstitutional on the grounds of its vagueness, not because it violated the Establishment Clause. He also pointed out that the rights of states to choose their curricula should not be infringed upon too readily. He also tried to draw a line between the kinds of teaching a state was entitled to determine and those it wasn't.[6]

> The States are most assuredly free "to choose their own curriculums for their own schools." A State is entirely free, for example, to decide that the only foreign language to be taught in its public school system shall be Spanish. But would a State be constitutionally free to punish a teacher for letting his students know that other languages are also spoken in the world? I think not.
>
> It is one thing for a State to determine that "the subject of higher mathematics, or astronomy, or biology" shall or shall not be included in its public school curriculum. It is quite another thing for a State to make it a criminal offense for a public school teacher so much as to mention the very existence of an entire system of respected human thought. That kind of criminal law, I think, would clearly impinge upon the guarantees of free communication contained in the First Amendment and made applicable to the States by the Fourteenth.
>
> The Arkansas Supreme Court has said that the statute before us may or may not be just such a law. The result, as MR. JUSTICE BLACK points out, is that "a teacher cannot know whether he is forbidden to mention Darwin's theory at all." Since I believe that no State could constitutionally forbid a teacher "to mention Darwin's theory at all," and since Arkansas may, or may not, have done just that, I conclude that the statute before us is so vague as to be invalid under the Fourteenth Amendment.

Justice Black made another interesting point about the idea that the theory of evolution was antireligious. If it were believed to be so, then wouldn't teaching it violate the idea that the state should be neutral between religion and nonreligion?

> A second question that arises for me is whether this Court's decision forbidding a State to exclude the subject of evolution from its schools infringes the religious freedom of those who consider evolution an anti-religious doctrine. If the theory is considered anti-religious, as the Court indicates, how can the State be bound by the Federal Constitution to permit its teachers to advocate such an "anti-religious" doctrine to school children? The very cases cited by the Court as supporting its conclusion hold that the State must be neutral, not favoring one religious or anti-religious view over another. The Darwinian theory is said to challenge the Bible's story of creation; so, too, have some of those who believe in the Bible, along with many others, challenged the

Darwinian theory. Since there is no indication that the literal Biblical doctrine of the origin of man is included in the curriculum of Arkansas schools, does not the removal of the subject of evolution leave the State in a neutral position toward these supposedly competing religious and anti-religious doctrines? *Unless this Court is prepared simply to write off as pure nonsense the views of those who consider evolution an anti-religious doctrine,* then this issue presents problems under the Establishment Clause far more troublesome than are discussed in the Court's opinion. (My italics)

Black makes an important point here. There is no question that the theory of evolution has serious negative consequences for some religious beliefs. In that sense, it is "antireligion." More generally, suppose a scientific theory flatly contradicts some religious belief. Doesn't teaching just that theory and not the opposing religious belief contradict the neutrality requirement of the Establishment Clause? Wouldn't neutrality require teaching both or omitting both?

Religious apologists who support science try to avoid this dilemma by arguing that scientific truths cannot be antireligious. There is only one truth, they argue, and any seeming contradiction between an established scientific theory and religious beliefs must be due to an erroneous interpretation of religion. This is what those who argue that science and religion are compatible say, dismissing as "pure nonsense," in Black's words, "the views of those who consider evolution an anti-religious doctrine."

But is it that straightforward? For example, suppose someone is convinced that science and religion are incompatible belief systems and that the more one appreciates the wonder of the scientific viewpoint and the power of methodological naturalism to determine the truths of the world, the less appeal the supernatural elements of religion will have. Is such a person's support for the teaching of more and better science necessarily also advocating an antireligious view and thus violating the neutrality requirement of the Establishment Clause?

The Supreme Court was able to reach a unanimous verdict in *Epperson* while avoiding having to resolve the particular question of whether allowing the teaching of a scientific theory that is considered antireligious, without balancing it with the teaching of the religious belief itself, violates the strict neutrality called for in the 1947 *Everson* ruling.

The *Epperson* verdict brought down the curtain on the first strategy of those opposing religion, ruling emphatically that states and their agencies could not ban the teaching of evolution in public schools. This set in motion the next act in the legal drama.

NOTES

1. Mano Singham, *Quest for Truth: Scientific Progress and Religious Beliefs* (Bloomington, IN: Phi Delta Kappan Educational Foundation, 2000), 4.

2. John Whitcomb and Henry M. Morris, *The Genesis Flood* (Phillipsburg, NJ: P&R Publishing, 1961).

3. Singham, *Quest for Truth*, 4.

4. *Epperson v. Arkansas*, 393 U.S. 97, www.law.cornell.edu/supct/html/historics/USSC_CR_0393_0097_ZO.html.

5. *Epperson v. Arkansas.* www.law.cornell.edu/supct/html/historics/USSC_CR_0393_0097_ZC.html.

6. *Epperson v. Arkansas.* www.law.cornell.edu/supct/html/historics/USSC_CR_0393_0097_ZC2.html.

Chapter 11

Adam and Eve
and Evolution

Following the defeat of attempts to ban the teaching of evolution in public schools, opponents of its teaching cast around for another way to combat its influence. This led to the idea of demanding "balance" in the classroom, so that the biblical theory of creation would be taught whenever evolution was.

But before those attempts wound their way through state legislatures, an important Supreme Court decision addressed Justice Hugo Black's concern expressed in *Epperson* as to whether allowing the teaching of a scientific theory that had a negative impact on religious beliefs meant that the government was acting against religion and thus violating its mandate of strict neutrality between religion and nonreligion.

The concerns Black raised were resolved three years later in the 1971 case of *Lemon v. Kurtzman*,[1] which set down guidelines for judging whether any law violated the Establishment Clause. Although this case did not deal directly with the teaching of evolution, it led to further clarification of this tricky issue and laid the groundwork for all future evolution cases.

The Lemon case bundled two separate cases together. One arose from a law passed in Rhode Island that provided "for a 15% salary supplement to be paid to teachers in nonpublic schools at which the average per-pupil expenditure on secular education is below the average in public schools. Eligible teachers must teach only courses offered in the public schools, using only materials used in the public schools, and must agree not to teach courses in religion."

The second case arose from challenges to a law passed in Pennsylvania that authorized the state superintendent of public instruction to "purchase" certain "secular educational services" from nonpublic schools, directly reimbursing those schools solely for teachers' salaries, textbooks, and instructional materials. Reimbursement was restricted to courses in specific secular subjects, the textbooks and materials had to be approved by the superintendent, and no payment was to be made for courses containing "any subject matter expressing religious teaching, or the morals or forms of worship of any sect."

In overturning both these laws by votes of 8–0 and 8–1, the Court promulgated the three-pronged "Lemon test," which holds that for any law to pass Establishment Clause constitutional muster, it must meet three criteria:

> First, the statute must have a secular legislative purpose (the purpose prong);
> Second, its principal or primary effect must be one that neither advances nor inhibits religion (the effect prong);
> Finally, the statute must not foster "an excessive government entanglement with religion" (the entanglement prong).

In other words, to satisfy the Establishment Clause, the *intent* of the law must have a secular basis. In addition, the fact that a law had the *incidental* effect of advancing or inhibiting religion did not automatically disqualify it. It also added a third criterion, requiring that the law must not result in the government getting too mixed up in the affairs of religion. The Court ruled that the Rhode Island and Pennsylvania policies would result in the states having detailed and complicated financial and other dealings with parochial schools, thus violating the entanglement prong.

The guidelines set out in *Lemon* addressed Black's concerns expressed in the Epperson case because, according to the Lemon test, even if a scientific theory like evolution undermines a religious belief, teaching just that theory and not the opposing religious belief does not violate the neutrality requirement of the Establishment Clause because teaching science has a clearly secular purpose since the goal of teaching science is to advance scientific knowledge and not to undermine religion. If religion happens to be undermined because of teaching a particular scientific theory like evolution, that is an incidental, not a primary, effect. By contrast, it would be unconstitutional to teach a theory whose *only purpose* or *primary effect* was to undermine or foster religion.

Faced with these strong majorities by the Supreme Court restricting the introduction of religion in schools, religious groups who opposed the teaching of evolution and wanted to introduce creationist alternatives into the science curriculum tried to find ways to do so that would (1) make creationism look scientific (thus meeting the needs of the purpose prong standard of the Lemon test), and (2) be at least neutral in their primary effects (thus meeting the effect prong standard).

Such groups felt that a creationist alternative to evolution could be inserted into the science curriculum by also appealing to the secular principle of "fairness." They argued that students should be taught both sides of any controversial issue as part of good teaching practice, thereby satisfying the neutrality requirement.

> Rather than seek the elimination of the teaching of evolution, a strategy that had not worked earlier, the emphasis now shifted to what was called a "balanced treatment" approach to the teaching of science. Creationists argued that the theory of evolution was just that, a "theory" and not a proven scientific fact. While conceding that this alone did not disqualify it from being taught in schools, they asserted that simple fairness demanded that other theories of life (such as creationism) that also had not been proven should be given equal time in the classroom. Students would then be able to evaluate for themselves which theory made the most sense. Creationists argued that, in addition to meeting the fairness criterion, such a balanced treatment would enhance critical thinking skills in students by encouraging them to think for themselves and make choices, rather than being told what to believe.[2]

An early attempt to adopt this strategy occurred in 1974 in the never-say-die state of Tennessee, which passed yet another law requiring that states give equal emphasis in their biology textbooks to alternative theories of origins, including the Genesis account. The law passed by the state said in Section 1,

> Any biology textbook used for teaching in the public schools, which expresses an opinion of, or relates a theory about origins or creation of man and his world shall be prohibited from being used as a textbook in such system unless it specifically states that it is a theory as to the origin and creation of man and his world and is not represented to be scientific fact. Any textbook so used in the public education system which expresses an opinion or relates to a theory or theories shall give in the same textbook and under the same subject commensurate attention to, and an equal amount of emphasis on, the origins and creation

of man and his world as the same is recorded in other theories, including, but not limited to, the Genesis account in the Bible.[3]

Of course, requiring the teaching of "other theories" of origins left the door wide open to the teaching of all manner of ideas aside from the Christian beliefs that were the intent of this legislation. So the legislators added a sentence that read, "The teaching of all occult or satanical beliefs of human origin is expressly excluded from this Act."

The writers of this legislation also tried to address another potential problem in that under this law, the use of the Bible might also be excluded since that book obviously contained a "theory about origins or creation of man and his world" and yet did not include other theories or carry the required disclaimer.

But they thought they could legislate their way out of that particular dilemma too. Since the above restrictions applied only to textbooks, they added another section to the law (Section 2), which said, "The Holy Bible shall not be defined as a textbook, but is hereby declared to be a reference work and shall not be required to carry the disclaimer above provided for textbooks."

The law was, of course, promptly challenged, and the case of *Daniel v. Waters*[4] went to trial. The problem was that by asking for the inclusion in the curriculum of an explicitly religious belief based on the Genesis account of the Bible, the legislators had stepped over the constitutional line. By that time, the Supreme Court had laid down so many fairly clear guidelines for adjudicating such cases that lower courts had little trouble determining that such an explicit appeal to include religious ideas in the public school curriculum violated the Establishment Clause of the First Amendment.

In a 2–1 ruling in 1975 striking down the Tennessee law as a violation of the Establishment Clause, the U.S. Sixth Court of Appeals said,

> We believe that in several respects *the statute under consideration is unconstitutional on its face*, that no state court interpretation of it can save it, and that in this case, the District Court clearly erred in abstaining from rendering a determination of the unconstitutionality of the statute on its face. . . .
>
> The result of this legislation is a clearly defined preferential position for the Biblical version of creation as opposed to any account of the development of man based on scientific research and reasoning. For a

state to seek to enforce such a preference by law is to seek to accomplish the very establishment of religion which the First Amendment to the Constitution of the United States squarely forbids. (My italics)

The legislators' attempt to keep out the work of Satan also backfired on them. The court ruled that the law ruling out the teaching of all "occult or satanical beliefs" violated the entanglement prong of the Lemon test because it would get the state involved in all kinds of messy theological disputes. "Throughout human history the God of some men has frequently been regarded as the Devil incarnate by men of other religious persuasions. It would be utterly impossible for the Tennessee Textbook Commission to determine which religious theories were 'occult' or 'satanical' without seeking to resolve the theological arguments which have embroiled and frustrated theologians through the ages."

Even the dissenting opinion was not based on sympathy for the statute; because the case had had a very complicated history, the judge simply felt that it was premature for the U.S. Sixth Court of Appeals to be judging the merits of the case.

This failed effort by Tennessee marked the end of the second phase of the struggle against the teaching of evolution. As a postscript to this episode, the ever-resilient people of Tennessee tried again in 1996 to pass legislation restricting teaching evolution in schools. That effort failed too, presumably because enough legislators realized by now that they were facing an uphill constitutional battle.[5]

NOTES

1. *Lemon v. Kurtzman*, 403 U.S. 602, www.law.cornell.edu/supct/html/historics/USSC_CR_0403_0602_ZO.html.

2. Mano Singham, *Quest for Truth: Scientific Progress and Religious Beliefs* (Bloomington, IN: Phi Delta Kappan Educational Foundation, 2000), 5.

3. *Daniel v. Waters*, 515 F.2d 485, www.talkorigins.org/faqs/daniel-v-waters.html.

4. *Daniel v. Waters*.

5. Edward J. Larson, *Summer for the Gods* (Cambridge, MA: Harvard University Press, 1997), 262.

Chapter 12

The Rise and Fall of "Creation Science"

The third phase of the antievolution struggle shifted from Tennessee to the neighboring states of Arkansas and Louisiana.

The advocates of religion, undeterred by their failure in Tennessee to insert biblical theories of creation into the science classroom, now sought to introduce those same religious ideas of creation into the biology curriculum in ways that would not violate the Establishment Clause.

From the Tennessee case they drew the lesson that any legislation aimed at achieving these goals had to be carefully worded so as to avoid any and all religious language or references to the Bible, yet expressed those biblical ideas in the language of science. From this effort emerged what is now known as "creation science," which had its basis in the ideas advanced in the book *The Genesis Flood* and was ostensibly a nonreligious alternative to the theory of evolution by natural selection.

On March 19, 1981, the governor of Arkansas signed into law Act 590, titled "Balanced Treatment for Creation-Science and Evolution-Science Act."[1] Its essential mandate is declared in its first sentence: "Public schools within this State shall give balanced treatment to creation-science and to evolution-science." The act stated, among other things, that "creation-science is an alternative *scientific model* of origins and can be presented from a *strictly scientific standpoint without any religious doctrine* just as evolution-science can, because there are scientists who conclude that scientific data best support creation-science and because scientific evidences and inferences have been presented for creation-science" (my italics).

Table 12.1.   Creation Science versus Evolution Science

"Creation science" includes the scientific evidences and related inferences that indicate the following:	"Evolution science" includes the scientific evidences and related inferences that indicate the following:
(1) Sudden creation of the universe, energy, and life from nothing	(1) Emergence by naturalistic processes of the universe from disordered matter and emergence of life from nonlife
(2) The insufficiency of mutation and natural selection in bringing about development of all living kinds from a single organism	(2) The sufficiency of mutation and natural selection in bringing about development of present living kinds from simple earlier kinds
(3) Changes only within fixed limits of originally created kinds of plants and animals	(3) Emergence by mutation and natural selection of present living kinds from simple earlier kinds
(4) Separate ancestry for man and apes	(4) Emergence of man from a common ancestor with apes
(5) Explanation of the earth's geology by catastrophism, including the occurrence of a worldwide flood	(5) Explanation of the earth's geology and the evolutionary sequence by uniformitarianism
(6) A relatively recent inception of the earth and living kinds	(6) An inception several billion years ago of the earth and somewhat later of life

Table 12.1 compares how the statute defined both "creation science" and "evolution science."

Notice that there are no explicit references to the Bible or religion or God in the definition of creation science, although the original source of the ideas behind them is quite obvious. Creation science is essentially biblical, young-Earth creationism, just using nonreligious language.

This law was, of course, challenged, and in 1982 in *McLean v. Arkansas Board of Education*,[2] U.S. District Court Judge William R. Overton declared the law unconstitutional. Despite its framers' careful efforts to craft language to make the law acceptable, the judge said that it failed to meet *all three prongs* of the Lemon test (purpose, effect, entanglement) for constitutionality under the Establishment Clause.

Discerning a law's intent or purpose is not straightforward, as Justice Hugo Black pointed out in his *Epperson* opinion, and courts take into account more than just the wording of the statute or what legislators *say* its intent is. As Judge Overton said, "Courts are not bound . . . by legislative statements of purpose or legislative disclaimers. In determining the legislative purpose of a statute, courts may consider evidence of the historical context of the Act, the specific sequence of events leading up to passage of the Act, departures from normal procedural sequences, substantive departures from the normal, and contemporaneous statements of the legislative sponsor."

In his ruling Judge Overton, using the testimony of philosopher of science Michael Ruse as a guide, tried to define science, saying,

> A descriptive definition was said to be that science is what is "accepted by the scientific community" and is "what scientists do.". . . More precisely, the essential characteristics of science are:
>   It is guided by natural law;
>   It has to be explanatory by reference to natural law;
>   It is testable against the empirical world;
>   Its conclusions are tentative, i.e. are not necessarily the final word; and
>   It is falsifiable.

The judge said that creation science failed to meet these criteria and thus was not science.

Many philosophers of science have criticized the judge's use of this definition of science (and the testimony of Ruse on which it was based), holding that it is not supported by the historical record of science.[3] They argue that while such a definition of science may have served the short-term purpose of keeping creationism out of science classrooms, making the definition of science into this kind of prescriptive list was not only unjustifiable on scholarly grounds but practically invited people to try to find new ways to insert religion into the curriculum by devising language to conform to this definition, while yet subverting science.

Some philosophers have argued that the problem with creation science, thus the reason it should not be taught, was that it was a *really bad theory*. But, of course, the Establishment Clause of the U.S. Constitution does not explicitly prohibit the teaching of any theories just because they are bad or discredited or even downright silly, raising once again the unresolved question of who should decide what should be taught in schools and what constraints, if any, apply to them.

Judge Overton added, "The creationists' methods do not take data, weigh it against the opposing scientific data, and thereafter reach the conclusions stated in Section 4(a). *Instead, they take the literal wording of the Book of Genesis and attempt to find scientific support for it. . . .* While anybody is free to approach a scientific inquiry in any fashion they choose, *they cannot properly describe the methodology as scientific, if they start with the conclusion and refuse to change it regardless of the evidence developed during the course of the investigation"* (my italics).

While Judge Overton's attempt to define science can be properly criticized, in the italicized passages he captures precisely why religion-based theories will never be considered science. In science, there is no external measure of truth (either from a book or revelation) that the results of your investigations must conform to. You have to go where the evidence leads you, even if the result is unpalatable to your religious, moral, or intellectual sensibilities.

Meanwhile, also in 1981, Louisiana had passed an act similar in spirit to the Arkansas one, called the "Balanced Treatment for Creation-Science and Evolution-Science in Public School Instruction Act."[4] This act said, "Commencing with the 1982–1983 school year, public schools within this state shall give balanced treatment to creation-science and to evolution-science." It further said that "balanced treatment" simply means "providing whatever information and instruction in both creation and evolution models the classroom teacher determines is necessary and appropriate to provide insight into both theories."

Louisiana's 1981 "balanced-treatment" act was less restrictive than Arkansas's. Unlike in Arkansas, where creation science was explicitly described in the statute itself, this statute's call to teach creation science merely meant talking about the "scientific evidences for creation and inferences from those scientific evidences," giving its backers hope that this vague language would help it pass muster constitutionally.

Not surprisingly, the Louisiana statute was also challenged and, like its Arkansas counterpart, ruled unconstitutional by a U.S. district court. The Louisiana verdict was then appealed to a federal appeals court, where the district court ruling was upheld by a narrow 8–7 margin.

The ghost of the Scopes trial emerged from the shadows again, as the federal appeals court panel said, when it made its ruling, "The case comes to us against a historical background that cannot be denied or ignored. . . . The Act continues the battle William Jennings Bryan carried to his grave. The Act's intended effect is to discredit evolution by counterbalancing its teaching at every turn with the teaching of creationism, a religious belief. The statute therefore is a law respecting a particular religious belief . . . and thus is unconstitutional."[5]

The advocates of teaching creation science, however, were not easily deterred. The narrowness of the margin in the appeals court must have given the law's supporters hope that the U.S. Supreme Court might overturn the verdict, and the appeals court ruling was appealed to the U.S. Supreme Court, making *Edwards v. Aguillard*, after *Epperson* in 1968, the second case dealing directly with the teaching of evolution in public schools to reach the highest judicial level.

But the hopes of creationists were dashed. In a landmark 1987 decision, the U.S. Supreme Court issued a 7–2 ruling (with Chief Justice William Rehnquist and Justice Antonin Scalia dissenting) holding the Louisiana statute unconstitutional because it violated the Establishment Clause. The decision said that the creation science legislation failed *all three* prongs of the Lemon test.

Since this decision plays a major role in the later development of what has come to be called "intelligent design theory" as the next vehicle to be used to undermine the teaching of evolution, it is worth quoting at length from the majority opinion written by Justice William Brennan.[6]

The Court first ruled that "creation science" was a religious belief; thus, the legislation was seeking to advance a religion.

> The preeminent purpose of the Louisiana Legislature was clearly to advance the religious viewpoint that a supernatural being created humankind. . . . The legislative history therefore reveals that the term "creation science," as contemplated by the legislature that adopted this Act, embodies the *religious belief that a supernatural creator was responsible for the creation of humankind*. . . .
>
> The Creationism Act is designed *either* to promote the theory of creation science which embodies a particular religious tenet by requiring that creation science be taught whenever evolution is taught

or to prohibit the teaching of a scientific theory disfavored by certain
religious sects by forbidding the teaching of evolution when creation
science is not also taught. . . . Because the primary purpose of the
Creationism Act is to advance a particular religious belief, the Act
endorses religion in violation of the First Amendment. (My italics)

Justice Brennan then dismissed the idea that forcing the teaching
of creation science, if evolution was taught, somehow served the
goal of academic freedom or enhancing "fairness."

It is equally clear that requiring schools to teach creation science with
evolution does not advance academic freedom. The Act does not grant
teachers a flexibility that they did not already possess to supplant the
present science curriculum with the presentation of theories, besides
evolution, about the origin of life. . . .

We find no merit in the State's argument that the "legislature may
not [have] use[d] the terms 'academic freedom' in the correct legal
sense. They might have [had] in mind, instead, a basic concept of fairness; teaching all of the evidence." . . .

Furthermore, the goal of basic "fairness" is hardly furthered by the
Act's discriminatory preference for the teaching of creation science
and against the teaching of evolution. While requiring that curriculum
guides be developed for creation science, the Act says nothing of comparable guides for evolution. Similarly, resource services are supplied
for creation science, but not for evolution. Only "creation scientists"
can serve on the panel that supplies the resource services. The Act
forbids school boards to discriminate against anyone who "chooses to
be a creation scientist" or to teach "creationism," but fails to protect
those who choose to teach evolution or any other non-creation-science
theory, or who refuse to teach creation science.

He then highlighted the basic problem that will forever bedevil
efforts to oppose or undermine the teaching of evolution. He said
that by singling out the theory of evolution for special treatment,
the legislation was *picking on the one major theory that history clearly
demonstrated had been opposed for religious reasons.*

If the Louisiana Legislature's purpose was solely to maximize the
comprehensiveness and effectiveness of science instruction, it would
have encouraged the teaching of all scientific theories about the origins
of humankind. But under the Act's requirements, teachers who were
once free to teach any and all facets of this subject are now unable to
do so. Moreover, the Act fails even to ensure that creation science will

be taught, but instead requires the teaching of this theory only when the theory of evolution is taught. Thus we agree with the Court of Appeals' conclusion that the Act does not serve to protect academic freedom, but has the distinctly different purpose of discrediting "evolution by counterbalancing its teaching at every turn with the teaching of creationism." . . .

In this case, the purpose of the Creationism Act was to restructure the science curriculum to conform with a particular religious viewpoint. *Out of many possible science subjects taught in the public schools, the legislature chose to affect the teaching of the one scientific theory that historically has been opposed by certain religious sects. . . .*

The legislative history documents that the Act's primary purpose was to change the science curriculum of public schools in order to provide persuasive advantage to a particular religious doctrine that rejects the factual basis of evolution in its entirety. (My italics)

The verdict in *Edwards* showed that the baggage of the historical record of religion-based efforts to undermine the teaching of evolution, starting with the Scopes trial, was too much to overcome. The Supreme Court had clearly determined that attempts to teach anything along the lines of "creation science" or to discredit evolution basically sprang from religious motivations; thus, any legislative attempts to mandate teaching such subject matter ran into the immediate presumption of failing both the purpose and effect prongs of the Lemon test, thereby violating the neutrality requirement set forth in the 1947 *Everson* ruling.

Following *Edwards v. Aguillard*, two other court cases that dealt with issues related to the teaching of evolution further narrowed the options available to opponents of that theory. In *Webster v. New Lenox School District*, the U.S. Seventh Court of Appeals ruled in 1990 that a teacher's free speech rights are not violated by a school district preventing him from teaching creation science, and in *Peloza v. Capistrano Unified School District*, the U.S. Ninth Court of Appeals in 1994 rejected the argument that "evolutionism" is a religion and thus requiring teachers to teach it violated the teacher's rights guaranteed under the First and Fourteenth Amendments.[7]

It is with this history of U.S. Supreme (and Appeals) Court decisions in mind that we can understand the emergence of the latest attempt to oppose the teaching of evolution. Despite the fact that they were facing such long odds, opponents of evolution now moved to stage four in their strategy. They understood the history of legal rulings as requiring that they avoid any explicitly religious language or ideas as well as mention of the Bible and that they avoid *mandating* the teaching of any particular theory.

All these judicial setbacks led to the adoption of efforts to undermine the credibility of the theory of evolution using the wedge of "intelligent design." This new theory was designed specifically to overcome the hurdles for constitutionality set by prior court rulings, especially those enunciated in *Edwards v. Aguillard*.

NOTES

1. See www.antievolution.org/projects/mclean/new_site/legal/act_590.htm.

2. *McLean v. Arkansas Board of Education*, 529 F. Supp. 1255, www.talkorigins.org/faqs/mclean-v-arkansas.html.

3. For a thorough airing of the philosophy of science issues raised in this trial, see Michael Ruse, ed., *But Is It Science?* (Amherst, NY: Prometheus Books, 1996). In particular, see chapter 21, "The Demise of the Demarcation Problem" by Larry Laudan.

4. See www.legis.state.la.us/lss/lss.asp?doc=80458.

5. Edward J. Larson, *Summer for the Gods* (Cambridge, MA: Harvard University Press, 1997), 259.

6. *Edwards v. Aguillard*, 482 U.S. 578, www.law.cornell.edu/supct/html/historics/USSC_CR_0482_0578_ZO.html.

7. Jeffrey P. Moran, *The Scopes Trial: A Brief History with Documents* (Boston, Mass.: Bedford/St. Martins, 2002), p. 217; *Webster v. New Lenox School District*, 917 F. 2d 1004, 1990, at http://cases.justia.com/us-court-of-appeals/F2/917/1003/350874/ and *Peloza v. Capistrano Unified School District* 37 F.3d 517, 1994, http://cases.justia.com/us-court-of-appeals/F3/37/517/509100/.

Chapter 13

Creation Science Born Again As Intelligent Design

"Intelligent design" (ID) can best be understood as a carefully crafted theory designed to eliminate those features that had led to the defeat (because of the Establishment Clause) of prior efforts to combat the teaching of evolution in public schools.

The fundamental goal of this new effort was the same as that sought since the time of the Scopes trial: to undermine or even eliminate the teaching of the theory of evolution and to bring back into schools a God-based view of creation. But, mindful of all the legal setbacks that previous efforts had met, ID advocates like Berkeley law professor Phillip Johnson tried to find new ways to make it acceptable to the courts. Johnson is considered the father of the intelligent design creationism movement, and his 1991 book *Darwin on Trial*[1] is usually taken as marking the origin of the idea.

The *Berkeley Science Review* describes the founding of the ID movement: "Two years later [i.e., 1993], Johnson organized a meeting at Pajaro Dunes near Monterey to bring like-minded thinkers together. Its participants would become the major public figures in intelligent design: Scott Minnich and Michael Behe, who would testify on behalf of ID in Dover, Steven Meyer, who would direct the Discovery Institute's Center for Science and Culture, and Jonathan Wells, who pursued a PhD in molecular and cell biology at Berkeley after becoming convinced that he 'should devote [his] life to destroying Darwinism.'"[2]

This group was well aware of the restrictions under which they had to operate. The succession of judicial rulings discussed earlier had drastically narrowed the range of options open to evolution's opponents. Bans on teaching evolution in public schools had been ruled out, and attempts to introduce explicitly religious ideas into the curriculum to balance evolution also had gone nowhere. Removing explicit references to religion and the Bible and requesting equal time for the resulting product, called "creation science," had not swayed the courts either.

This did not leave religious advocates with much room to maneuver. People who wanted to bring God back into the classroom realized that doing so would require a much subtler and more sophisticated strategy than those that had been tried before.

First, they had to disown any connection with all earlier efforts so that legislative history could not be used against them. In particular, this meant avoiding at all costs being associated with the "creationist" label, which had already been tainted as identified with one particular religious view, and the courts had rejected teaching that view as violating the Establishment Clause. Being considered an offshoot of creationism was seen as the kiss of death as far as constitutional acceptability went.

In *Edwards v. Aguillard*, the court had made this point quite clearly: "The Act impermissibly endorses religion by advancing the religious belief that a supernatural being created humankind. The legislative history demonstrates that the term 'creation science,' as contemplated by the state legislature, embraces this religious teaching."

ID advocates realized that they needed a strategy that would never even mention the Bible or God or Christianity or creationism or creation science, or even require the teaching of any alternative theories to evolution, since that too had been seen as constitutionally suspect.

The only option that remained was to seek to discredit the theory of evolution by undermining its credibility. In order to do this, two of the original ID strategists, Michael Behe[3] and Jonathan Wells,[4] each wrote a book targeting evolution and alleging that the theory had fatal weaknesses. These books would become almost the sacred texts of the ID movement. Wells's book follows up the theme of a 1978 book by Duane Gish,[5] which also sought to highlight the alleged weaknesses of evolution.

(It is noteworthy that the ID movement umbrella covers a wide spectrum of religious believers, with Behe being a Roman Catholic, Wells a member of the Unification Church of Reverend Sun Myung Moon, and Gish a Baptist.)

Jonathan Wells (b. 1946), a strong advocate of intelligent design and a fellow of the Discovery Institute, became a member of Reverend Sun Myung Moon's Unification Church, graduating from its theological seminary. The church then sponsored him for a PhD in religious studies in 1978. Convinced that the theory of evolution was wrong and determined to dethrone it from its dominance in science, he obtained a PhD in 1994 in embryology from the University of California, Berkeley, in order to better equip himself to fight it. He is the author of *Icons of Evolution: Science or Myth? How Much of What We Teach about Evolution Is Wrong* (2000), which intelligent design advocates quote widely.

Of course, such a minimalist strategy of merely discrediting the theory of evolution by natural selection fell far short of fundamentalist religious people's goal of bringing prayer, Bible readings, and the Genesis story back into the schools. Furthermore, the ID movement has always consisted of just a very few people. It needed the sheer numbers and the political and economic support of the much more numerous religious fundamentalists. Thus, the movement had to do some delicate maneuvering, balancing the legal need to avoid

Duane Gish (b. 1921), a biochemist, received his PhD from the University of California, Berkeley, in 1953. He is a creationist and former vice president of the Institute of Creation Research founded by Henry Morris. He believes that the creation story in the book of Genesis is a historical fact and that all scientific evidence can be interpreted to support that belief. A well-practiced polemicist, his best-known book is *Evolution: The Fossils Say No!* (1978), which he followed up with *Evolution? The Fossils Still Say No!* (1995). He is a Baptist.

seeming to have anything to do with religion, while at the same time reassuring religious believers that intelligent design was indeed a way of getting religion back in the schools.

As a result there developed an elaborate and carefully choreographed dance, consisting of nods and winks and nudges, to convince the faithful that the ID movement was merely the vanguard designed to get the religious nose into the tent of the schools. Once that was achieved, once the wall of separation in the Establishment Clause had been breached in this way, other more overtly religious practices could be slowly reintroduced.

This strategy was fully laid out in an ID internal document known, appropriately enough, as the "Wedge strategy."

NOTES

1. Phillip Johnson, *Darwin on Trial* (Washington, DC: Regnery, 1991).

2. Michelangelo D'Agostino, *In the matter of Berkeley v. Berkeley*, Berkeley Science Review, Spring 2006, http://sciencereview.berkeley.edu/articles/issue10/evolution.pdf.

3. Michael Behe, *Darwin's Black Box* (New York: Free Press, 1996).

4. Jonathan Wells, *Icons of Evolution* (Washington, DC: Regnery, 2000).

5. Duane Gish, *Evolution: The Fossils Say No!* (Green Forest, AZ: Master Books, 1978).

Chapter 14

Why Some Hate Evolution: The Wedge Document Revelations

To understand how the theory of intelligent design creationism came into being, its essential idea, and the motivations of the people behind it, one needs to understand why there is such a deep-seated opposition to Darwin's theory of evolution by natural selection, especially in the United States.

Although, as stated earlier, the lack of directionality and purpose in the natural selection process was intellectually disturbing to those who wished to see human beings as somehow special, the almost visceral dislike of the theory in more recent times has its roots in social and political developments starting around the mid-twentieth century.

On the surface, ID seems to accept (or at least leave unchallenged) almost all of the key elements of evolutionary theory, such as the nonconstancy of species (the basic idea of evolution), the descent of all organisms (including humans) from common ancestors (branching evolution), the multiplication of species, and an old Earth.

So how was ID to advance the cause of religion if it seemed to accept so many evolutionary ideas that had been deemed to be hostile to it? The strategy is explicitly outlined in an internal document that has been labeled the "Wedge strategy" or the "Wedge document,"[1] created in 1998 by the Center for Science and Culture[2] of the Seattle-based Discovery Institute,[3] the well-funded think tank that funds and supports the work of intelligent design creationists.

This document came to light fairly recently and showed the religious motivations of those behind ID, despite their protestations to the contrary and public disavowals of any religious intent. It reveals an apocalyptic mind set that sees a catastrophic future for America unless evolutionary thinking is overthrown and God restored to a position of primacy in schools and other public spaces. The strategy outlined in its pages reveals ambitions that extend far beyond the narrow goal of fighting the teaching of evolution in schools. That particular battle is viewed as a mere skirmish, a prelude to a much bigger war believed to have momentous consequences.[4]

Here is an extended passage from the introduction section of the document that outlines the grand strategy to deal with the issues as seen by ID proponents:

> The proposition that human beings are created in the image of God is one of the bedrock principles on which Western civilization was built. Its influence can be detected in most, if not all, of the West's greatest achievements, including representative democracy, human rights, free enterprise, and progress in the arts and sciences.
>
> Yet a little over a century ago, this cardinal idea came under wholesale attack by intellectuals drawing on the discoveries of modern science. Debunking the traditional conceptions of both God and man, thinkers such as Charles Darwin, Karl Marx, and Sigmund Freud *portrayed humans not as moral and spiritual beings, but as animals or machines who inhabited a universe ruled by purely impersonal forces and whose behavior and very thoughts were dictated by the unbending forces of biology, chemistry, and environment.* This *materialistic conception of reality* eventually infected virtually every area of our culture, from politics and economics to literature and art.
>
> The cultural consequences of this triumph of materialism were devastating. Materialists denied the existence of objective moral standards, claiming that environment dictates our behavior and beliefs. Such moral relativism was uncritically adopted by much of the social sciences, and it still undergirds much of modern economics, political science, psychology and sociology.
>
> Materialists also undermined personal responsibility by asserting that human thoughts and behaviors are dictated by our biology and environment. The results can be seen in modern approaches to criminal justice, product liability, and welfare. In the materialist scheme of things, everyone is a victim and no one can be held accountable for his or her actions.
>
> Finally, materialism spawned a virulent strain of utopianism. Thinking they could engineer the perfect society through the application of scientific knowledge, materialist reformers advocated coercive government programs that falsely promised to create heaven on earth.

Discovery Institute's Center for the Renewal of Science and Culture *seeks nothing less than the overthrow of materialism and its cultural legacies.* (My italics)

A little later in the Wedge document, one comes across the movement's "governing goals," which are

- to defeat scientific materialism and its destructive moral, cultural, and political legacies
- to replace materialistic explanations with the theistic understanding that nature and human beings are created by God

So the goals of the ID movement are clear and reveal an almost apocalyptic mind set. The group takes aim at what followers see as the source of all evil: the idea that *materialism is the basis of all knowledge.* They feel that if they can displace materialism as an operating principle, then they can hope to eventually bring back nonmaterial entities into the schools as an acceptable explanation of phenomena, opening the way for the eventual return of God.

ID proponents feel that the working principle in science of *methodological naturalism* (the assumption that when one is seeking an explanation for any physical phenomenon, one should limit oneself to purely natural explanations and exclude the supernatural) is pernicious and antireligious and should be overthrown. ID strategist William Dembski in 2002 explicitly laid out this particular goal of the ID movement when he said,[5]

So long as methodological naturalism sets the ground rules for how the game of science is to be played, IDT [intelligent design theory] has no chance [in] Hades. . . . In the words of Vladimir Lenin, *What is to be done*? Design theorists aren't at all bashful about answering this question: *The ground rules of science have to be changed.* We need to realize that methodological naturalism is the functional equivalent of a full-blown metaphysical naturalism. Metaphysical naturalism asserts that the material world is all there is (in the words of Carl Sagan, "the cosmos is all there ever was, is, or will be").

These religious people strongly oppose Charles Darwin's theory because they see him, along with Sigmund Freud and Karl Marx, as the cofounder of a materialist philosophy that has led, in their view, to the degeneration of modern Western society. They see the elimination of prayer and other Christian activities in schools as the proximate cause of that decline and the reversal of that trend as the first step in bringing society back to some imagined earlier glory. Of the three named villains, Darwin is the obvious target to start with since his ideas are seen as the most pernicious, while the works of the other two do not have quite the same paradigmatic status and are not taught in schools.

The Discovery Institute's long-term strategy seems to be first to undermine the fundamental materialist idea of evolution by natural selection by allowing for the possibility of nonmaterial causation for at least some evolutionary changes, then later to introduce something they call "intelligent design" as an alternative to the undermined theory of evolution, then to bring God back into science education as an explanation for the origin of at least some species, and finally to put God, the Bible, and prayer back into public schools everywhere, thereby saving the world from sin. They see this as a goal that will be slowly and incrementally achieved, taking many years.

They have tried to undermine Darwinian thinking by discrediting one key idea of Darwinian natural selection, gradualism, which as-

Intelligent Design

The theory of intelligent design holds that certain features of the universe and of living things are best explained by an intelligent cause, not an undirected process such as natural selection. . . .

Intelligent design begins with the observation that intelligent agents produce complex and specified information (CSI). Design theorists hypothesize that if a natural object was designed, it will contain high levels of CSI. Scientists then perform experimental tests upon natural objects to determine if they contain complex and specified information. One easily testable form of CSI is irreducible complexity, which can be discovered by experimentally reverse-engineering biological structures to see if they require all of their parts to function.

—From www.intelligentdesign.org/whatisid.php.

serts that all changes in organisms occur over long periods by means of tiny, incremental, and random steps, with just those individuals having a survival advantage increasing their numbers in future generations.

ID proponents argue that there are a few biological systems of so-called irreducible complexity (the bacterial flagellum, the blood-clotting mechanism, and the human immune system being invoked most often) whose appearance cannot be explained by such a gradual process and thus must have nonmaterial causes. This is the fundamental tenet of intelligent design.

Along the way, they point to other alleged failures of evolution-ary theory to explain certain facts. A popular topic in intelligent design literature is the alleged mystery of the Cambrian explosion revealed in the Burgess Shale deposits in the Rocky Mountains in British Columbia in Canada. Excavations in this area unearthed a rich diversity of fossils, some of them soft-bodied, that seemed to "suddenly" appear (at least in terms of geological time scales) about five hundred million years ago.

The ID people suggest that this too could not have occurred by the normal gradual processes demanded by natural selection theory and hints at some other forces at work. But evolutionary paleobi-ologists like Simon Conway Morris who have studied the fossils in depth argue that there is nothing mysterious about their appearance at all.[6]

Meanwhile, many scientists have pointed out that the arguments of intelligent design advocates are not sustainable by the evidence. Niall Shanks[7] and Kenneth Miller[8] (among many others) have closely examined all their biological and mathematical arguments and found them seriously flawed.

Despite the scientific community's deep skepticism about their ideas, the ID movement crafted its strategy quite carefully so that it was making some progress. As part of this strategy, advocates care-fully avoided talk of God as much as possible (at least in public). Encountering strenuous opposition to the idea of including ID in the science curriculum, after a few years they began insisting that they did not favor teaching intelligent design in schools after all. Instead they adopted the strategy of requiring the acknowledgment that evolution was "just a theory," that it could not explain some things, that there was a controversy over some of its basic tenets, and that good science and teaching practice required that students be exposed to the nature of this alleged controversy.

Burgess Shale Deposit

Charles Doolittle Walcott (1850–1927), then secretary of the Smithsonian Institution, was a paleontologist who stumbled upon the Burgess Shale soft-bodied fossil deposits in 1909 while traveling on horseback with his wife and son along the ridge that connects Mount Field and Wapta Mountain in British Columbia, Canada. Although it is now known that the soil conditions that enabled the preservation of such fossils are not unique to the Burgess Shale area and have been found elsewhere, the scientific sensation created by the original discovery of such fossils has given this site a special significance. (Simon Conway Morris, *The Crucible of Creation*, Oxford: Oxford University Press, 1998).

It is easy to imagine how an avalanche of fine mud sliding down from the submerged reef top would have carried off any animals living in the shallow reef waters above. This avalanche could have caught some animals in mid-water and certainly would have overwhelmed and buried any creatures living at its base. The hard parts of all these animals caught in the mudslide were preserved as fossils, like the process at any other Cambrian site. However, here the fine mud also penetrated and filled all available spaces within the animals, thus preserving the shapes and locations of all the soft parts. This is a rare event and has made these fossils extremely valuable to the paleontologist.

—From "The Burgess Shale Site 510 Million Years Ago," Smithsonian Museum of Natural History, http:// paleobiology.si.edu/burgess/cambrianWorld.html

They managed to get supporters elected to state school boards in Kansas and Ohio, who then inserted into their state science standards ID-inspired language critical of evolution and the underlying scientific principle of methodological naturalism. In 2002, they also got Georgia's Cobb County to insert stickers in students' biology textbooks asserting that evolution was only a theory and not a fact.

> This textbook contains material on evolution. Evolution is a theory, not a fact, regarding the origin of living things. This material should be approached with an open mind, studied carefully, and critically considered.
>
> **Approved by**
> **Cobb County Board of Education**
> **Thursday, March 28, 2002**

Knowing that eventually someone would challenge the use of ID ideas in schools in the courts, ID advocates carefully avoided any actions or words that could, based on legal precedents, be interpreted as Establishment Clause violations. Their whole approach was to run a stealth campaign, essentially based on a public relations strategy.

This minimalist stealth approach caused some tension within the religious community since many religious people did not quite understand it. Many fundamentalist Christians are militantly proud of their faith and do not feel at all apologetic about their attempts to kick evolution out of the science curriculum and to put God back in the classroom where, they feel, he rightfully belongs. They are proud of being Christians and view the United States as a Christian country. They perceived the ID strategists' delicate maneuvering not as a constitutionally astute strategy but as somewhat cowardly. They wanted nothing to do with Darwinian theory *in any form* and saw the ID strategy of accepting most of its elements as needlessly accommodating of anti-Christian beliefs.

Furthermore, there is also a wide divergence in religious beliefs under the big religious tent. The more sophisticated ID theorists, like Michael Behe, say they accept most ideas about evolution, including a very old Earth, a common ancestor for humans and apes, and so on. This created underlying tensions between them and young-Earth biblical literalists, who emphatically reject such ideas and are the most passionate and vocal in their opposition to evolution.

When I attended various ID meetings and conferences in 2002 and 2003 as an invited speaker to argue why intelligent design did not belong in the science classroom, I found a huge gulf between the ID strategists, who were the featured speakers, and the rank-and-file attendees. The latter were largely fundamentalist, young-Earth Christians who took the Bible literally and did not speak the sophisticated language of the ID theorists.

These people had a much simpler view of the world. In their eyes, the United States was rapidly going to hell. Everywhere they looked, they saw signs of increasing decadence: more nudity, sex, pornography, abortion, crime, violence, profanity, blasphemy, and so on. They saw this as a direct consequence of removing God and prayer from the schools and teaching "Godless evolution," which said that we were no better than monkeys. It did not seem to occur to them that the "golden age" they wistfully looked back on was also a time of genocide, slavery, oppression of minorities, and overt discrimination of all kinds, hardly a state we would desire to return to.

So, while all these diverse religious elements agreed on the ultimate goal of removing the teaching of evolution from schools, the religiously naïve wanted to mount a direct assault to bring religion back into the classroom, while the more sophisticated ID strategists felt that one needed to proceed much more cautiously and stealthily, by first subtly undermining the idea that materialist explanations were the only ones allowed in science, and then, once that had been established, introducing more overtly religious ideas.

For about a decade, these differences and tensions within the religious community about how best to deal with the alleged Darwinian menace stayed hidden from public view. It took the Dover trial to draw back the curtain and bring the disagreements completely out into the open.

NOTES

1. See www.antievolution.org/features/wedge.html.
2. See www.discovery.org/csc.
3. See www.discovery.org.
4. For a comprehensive analysis of the "Wedge strategy," see Barbara Forrest and Paul R. Gross, *Creationism's Trojan Horse: The Wedge of Intelligent Design* (Oxford: Oxford University Press, 2004).
5. William A. Dembski, *What every theologian should know about creation, evolution and design*, www.origins.org/articles/dembski_theologn.html.
6. Simon Conway Morris, *The Crucible of Creation* (Oxford: Oxford University Press, 1998).
7. Niall Shanks, *God, the Devil, and Darwin* (Oxford: Oxford University Press, 2004).
8. Kenneth R. Miller, *Finding Darwin's God* (New York: Harper Collins, 1999).

Chapter 15

The Endorsement Test and the "Informed, Reasonable Observer"

Before the Dover trial tested the ideas of intelligent design and its supporters' attempts to undermine the teaching of evolution in 2005, several other important nonevolution cases took place whose rulings influenced the outcome in *Dover*.

One was an Establishment Clause case not directly related to religion in schools but with implications for it. It was the 1989 case *County of Allegheny v. ACLU*,[1] in which some citizens challenged the practice of displaying a crèche and a menorah in front of the county courthouse at Christmas time. In a 5–4 ruling, the U.S. Supreme Court said that displaying the crèche was unconstitutional but the Menorah was allowed.

In his majority opinion, Justice Harry Blackmun reiterated the belief that the government must be secular and addressed the issue of whether denying Christians the right to display their religious symbols was, in effect, favoring nonbelievers.

The Constitution mandates that the government remain secular, rather than affiliate itself with religious beliefs or institutions, precisely in order to avoid discriminating among citizens on the basis of their religious faiths. . . .

For this reason, the claim that prohibiting government from celebrating Christmas as a religious holiday discriminates against Christians in favor of nonadherents must fail. . . .

In contrast, confining the government's own celebration of Christmas to the holiday's secular aspects does not favor the religious beliefs of non-Christians over those of Christians. Rather, it simply permits the government to acknowledge the holiday without expressing an allegiance to

Why the Public Display of a Menorah Isn't Unconstitutional

The display of the Chanukah menorah in front of the City-County Building may well present a closer constitutional question. The menorah, one must recognize, is a religious symbol: it serves to commemorate the miracle of the oil as described in the Talmud. But the menorah's message is not exclusively religious. The menorah is the primary visual symbol for a holiday that, like Christmas, has both religious and secular dimensions.

Moreover, the menorah here stands next to a Christmas tree and a sign saluting liberty. While no challenge has been made here to the display of the tree and the sign, their presence is obviously relevant in determining the effect of the menorah's display. The necessary result of placing a menorah next to a Christmas tree is to create an "overall holiday setting" that represents both Christmas and Chanukah—two holidays, not one.

The mere fact that Pittsburgh displays symbols of both Christmas and Chanukah does not end the constitutional inquiry. If the city celebrates both Christmas and Chanukah as religious holidays, then it violates the Establishment Clause. The simultaneous endorsement of Judaism and Christianity is no less constitutionally infirm than the endorsement of Christianity alone.

Conversely, if the city celebrates both Christmas and Chanukah as secular holidays, then its conduct is beyond the reach of the Establishment Clause. Because government may celebrate Christmas as a secular holiday, it follows that government may also acknowledge Chanukah as a secular holiday. Simply put, it would be a form of discrimination against Jews to allow Pittsburgh to celebrate Christmas as a cultural tradition while simultaneously disallowing the city's acknowledgment of Chanukah as a contemporaneous cultural tradition.

> Accordingly, the relevant question for Establishment Clause purposes is whether the combined display of the tree, the sign, and the menorah has the effect of endorsing both Christian and Jewish faiths, or rather simply recognizes that both Christmas and Chanukah are part of the same winter holiday season, which has attained a secular status in our society. Of the two interpretations of this particular display, the latter seems far more plausible, and is also in line with *Lynch.*
>
> The Christmas tree, unlike the menorah, is not itself a religious symbol. Although Christmas trees once carried religious connotations, today they typify the secular celebration of Christmas. . . .
>
> Although the city has used a symbol with religious meaning as its representation of Chanukah, this is not a case in which the city has reasonable alternatives that are less religious in nature. It is difficult to imagine a predominantly secular symbol of Chanukah that the city could place next to its Christmas tree.
>
> —From the majority opinion of Justice Harry Blackmun
> (*County of Allegheny v. ACLU*)

Christian beliefs, an allegiance that would truly favor Christians over non-Christians. To be sure, some Christians may wish to see the government proclaim its allegiance to Christianity in a religious celebration of Christmas, but the Constitution does not permit the gratification of that desire, which would contradict the "the logic of secular liberty" it is the purpose of the Establishment Clause to protect.

Although the close vote in this case may have initially given some hope to religious groups, even the minority opinion reiterated the strong basic consensus that the government should not be in the position of seeming to favor one religion. It simply disagreed with this specific verdict, arguing that the crèche was merely a passive symbol reflecting the heritage of the nation and unlikely to lead to the establishment of a state religion.

In his dissent, Justice Anthony Kennedy said,[2]

> The Establishment Clause permits government some latitude in recognizing and accommodating the central role religion plays in our society. Any approach less sensitive to our heritage would border on latent hostility toward religion, as it would require government, in all its multifaceted roles, to acknowledge only the secular, to the exclusion and so to the detriment of the religious. . . .
>
> Our cases disclose two limiting principles: government may not coerce anyone to support or participate in any religion or its exercise; and it may not, in the guise of avoiding hostility or callous indifference, give direct benefits to religion in such a degree that it, in fact, "establishes a [state] religion or religious faith, or tends to do so."

So, although this case did not involve evolution, it again strongly endorsed the principle that the government should practice strict neutrality when it comes to matters of religion.

In 2000, another case involving religion in schools but not directly addressing evolution reached the U.S. Supreme Court. This was *Santa Fe Independent School District v. Doe*,[3] which challenged a school district's practice of having a student who had been elected the high school's student council chaplain deliver a prayer over the public address system before each home varsity football game.

The Court ruled 6–3 that such prayers were unconstitutional. In its ruling, the Court relied on an alternative formulation of the effect prong of the Lemon test articulated by Justice Sandra Day O'Connor in the 1984 case of *Lynch v. Donnelly*[4] involving the display of a nativity scene by a municipality.

In *Lynch*, O'Connor articulated what is now called the "endorsement test," writing, "The second and more direct infringement [of the establishment clause] is government endorsement or disapproval of religion. Endorsement sends a message to nonadherents that they are outsiders, not full members of the political community, and an accompanying message to adherents that they are insiders, favored members of the political community. Disapproval sends the opposite message."

Writing for the majority in the 2000 Santa Fe case, Justice John Paul Stevens used that language to overrule the policy of student-led prayer at football games, thus extending the reach of the endorsement test to school settings as well. "School sponsorship of a religious message is impermissible because it sends the ancillary

---

Lemon test

Every analysis in this area must begin with consideration of the cumulative criteria developed by the Court over many years. Three such tests may be gleaned from our cases. First, the statute must have a secular legislative purpose; second, its principal or primary effect must be one that neither advances nor inhibits religion; finally, the statute must not foster "an excessive government entanglement with religion."

—From the majority opinion of Chief Justice Warren E. Burger in the case of *Lemon v. Kurtzman.*

---

message to members of the audience who are nonadherents 'that they are outsiders, not full members of the political community, and an accompanying message to adherents that they are insiders, favored members of the political community.'"

O'Connor's formulation of the endorsement test and the *Santa Fe* precedent played important roles in the reasoning underlying the later *Dover* verdict.

Another important Establishment Clause case also did not deal explicitly with evolution. It was the much publicized 2004 *Elk Grove Unified School District v. Newdow*[5] in which a parent, Michael Newdow, challenged his daughter's school's including the phrase "under God" in the Pledge of Allegiance. The U.S. District Court ruled against him, but this was overruled by the Ninth Circuit Court of Appeals, which found in his favor. The case was then appealed to the U.S. Supreme Court.

The Supreme Court reversed the appeals court verdict 8–0 but on mixed grounds (Justice Antonin Scalia did not take part in the case). A majority of five justices said that due to a family dispute over whether the father or mother had custody of the child and therefore the standing to sue, the courts had no jurisdiction to review the case. Thus, they did not go into the merits of deciding whether including the phrase "under God" in schools was constitutional or not. Justices William Rehnquist, Sandra Day O'Connor, and Clarence Thomas agreed with the verdict overturning the appeals court decision but said that the Supreme Court should have reviewed the case on the merits. They then proceeded to do so and said that the practice was constitutional.

In her concurring opinion on the ruling, Justice O'Connor introduced an important new element. She said the decision on whether the government is involved in an impermissible endorsement of religion must be made from the viewpoint of a "reasonable observer" who "must embody a community ideal of social judgment, as well as rational judgment" and who "does not evaluate a practice in isolation from its origins and context. Instead, the reasonable observer must be deemed aware of the history of the conduct in question, and must understand its place in our Nation's cultural landscape."[6]

As we will see, this idea of using an informed and reasonable observer as the standard by which to judge whether an endorsement of religion has occurred also played a significant role in the *Dover* verdict.

A case that did deal with evolution arose in 2002 when a school board in Cobb County, Georgia, inserted stickers into students' biology textbooks, informing them, "This textbook contains material on evolution. Evolution is a theory, not a fact, regarding the origin of living things. This material should be approached with an open mind, studied carefully, and critically considered."

The sticker policy was challenged, and in January 2005, in *Selman v. Cobb County School District*,[7] U.S. District Court Judge Clarence Cooper ruled the policy unconstitutional, again applying the Lemon test.

Cooper first said that the sticker policy passed the purpose prong of the Lemon test:

> After considering the additional arguments and evidence presented by the parties and evaluating the evidence in light of the applicable law, the Court remains convinced that the Sticker at issue serves at least two secular purposes. First, the Sticker fosters critical thinking by encouraging students to learn about evolution and to make their own assessment regarding its merit. Second, by presenting evolution in a manner that is not unnecessarily hostile, the Sticker reduces offense to students and parents whose beliefs may conflict with the teaching of evolution. For the foregoing reasons, the Court concludes that the Sticker satisfies the first prong of the *Lemon* analysis.

However, he said that the sticker failed the effect prong, making it unconstitutional; thus, the stickers had to be removed. As part of his justification, he combined Justice Stevens's language about endorsement in the 2000 Santa Fe case and Justice O'Connor's assertion in the 2004 Elk Grove case that the relevant standard of judgment in such cases is how a knowledgeable and reasonable observer might perceive an action. "In this case, the Court believes that an informed, reasonable observer would interpret the Sticker to convey a message of endorsement of religion. That is, the Sticker sends a message to those who oppose evolution for religious reasons that they are favored members of the political community, while the Sticker sends a message to those who believe in evolution that they are political outsiders."

This decision was appealed by the school board, and in May 2006, the U.S. Court of Appeals for the Eleventh Circuit vacated Judge Cooper's decision,[8] not because it disagreed with the verdict itself but because it found that the record on appeal was incomplete. The appeals court said that it would "leave it to the district court whether to start with an entirely clean slate and a completely new trial or to supplement, clarify, and flesh out the evidence that it has heard in the four days of bench trial already conducted." But on December 19, 2006, the Cobb County School Board settled the case by agreeing to remove all the stickers,[9] thus ending that case in favor of the supporters of evolution.

None of these trials involved intelligent design, but all these legal precedents set the stage for the most recent and highly publicized court battle over the teaching of evolution in which ID first came under direct legal scrutiny. This occurred somewhat unexpectedly in Dover, Pennsylvania, in 2005 in the case of *Kitzmiller v. Dover Area School District*, presided over by U.S. District Judge John E. Jones III.

NOTES

1. *County of Allegheny v. ACLU*, 492 U.S. 573, www.law.cornell.edu/supct/html/historics/USSC_CR_0492_0573_ZO.html.

2. *County of Allegheny v. ACLU*. www.law.cornell.edu/supct/html/historics/USSC_CR_0492_0573_ZX2.html.

3. *Santa Fe Independent School District v. Doe*, 530 U.S. 290, www.law.cornell.edu/supct/html/historics/USSC_CR_0530_0290_ZO.html.

4. *Lynch v. Donnelly*, 465 U.S. 668, www.law.cornell.edu/supct/html/historics/USSC_CR_0465_0668_ZC.html.

5. *Elk Grove Unified School District v. Newdow*, 542 U.S. 1, www.law.cornell.edu/supct/html/02-1624.ZO.html.

6. *Elk Grove Unified School District v. Newdow*. www.law.cornell.edu/supct/html/historics/USSC_CR_0492_0573_ZC1.html.

7. *Selman v. Cobb County School District*, 102-CV-2325-CCfaqs/cobb/selman-v-cobb.html.

8. See www.ca11.uscourts.gov/opinions/ops/200510341.pdf.

9. *Americans United Applauds Settlement Of Georgia Lawsuit Over Evolution Disclaimer*, Press Release issued by Americans United for Separation of Church and State, Tuesday, December 19, 2006, http://www.au.org/site/News2?abbr=pr&page=NewsArticle&id=8797&security=1002&news_iv_ctrl=1241.

Chapter 16

The *Dover* Policy on Teaching Evolution

As we have seen, intelligent design creationism strategists had laid out a careful long-term stealth strategy aimed at discrediting the theory of evolution and undermining the scientific principle of methodological naturalism, with the goal of eventually breaking through the "wall of separation" that excluded religious instruction from public schools because of the Establishment Clause in the First Amendment. They should have heeded the warning of Scottish poet Robert Burns, who in his poem "To a Mouse" cautioned those who place too much faith in detailed plans for the future:

> The best laid schemes o' Mice an' Men,
> Gang aft a-gley

During the events in Dover, Pennsylvania, the carefully thought-out plans and strategy of the ID movement ganged agley in a big way, precisely because of the unresolved tensions within the religious community, which caused the sophisticated and long-term strategy of ID theorists to run aground on the rocks of the passions of their less sophisticated but more traditionally religious supporters.

In many ways, the Dover trial was a fitting bookend to the Scopes trial. I mentioned earlier that the Scopes trial had more features of a comedy than of a drama, and so did the Dover case. As in the Scopes trial, a colorful cast of local characters impulsively waded into a swirling national debate and completely muddied the waters. As in *Scopes*, a trial taking place in a small town received huge national and even international coverage.

God or Gorilla

by Matthew Chapman

I did not know much about evolution, but a quick study of the subject showed that 99 percent of scientists believed in it. Why would one doubt them? Did the pedestrian question the theory of gravity? Did the farmer who went to the doctor question his diagnosis? Why in this one area of science did nonexperts feel compelled to disagree with those who clearly knew better? . . .

I . . . discovered that many Americans not only rejected the theory of evolution; they reviled it. . . . By this time, it was public knowledge that I was an offspring of Darwin, and . . . it became apparent to me, really for the first time, how hated the poor old codger is. People such as [local preacher Reverend] Groves believe that Darwin marks a point in history from which materialism sprang, bringing with it Hitler, Stalin, Pol Pot, pot, sex, prostitution, abortion, homosexuality, and everything else nasty in the world.

It occurred to me how lucky we are that Darwin lived such a dull monogamous life. Had he been an adulterer, his theory would be dead and buried. Or maybe not. Joseph Smith, a contemporary of Darwin's and the polygamous founder of the Mormons, simply stated that his "truth" was handed to him on a set of golden plates that then mysteriously disappeared. Perhaps if Darwin had done the same he'd have avoided all this controversy.

—From *Harper's Magazine*, February 2006.

Someone (Matthew Chapman) even played the role of the detached and amused observer filled by reporter H. L. Mencken in *Scopes*.[1] To add to the strong sense of history, Chapman also happens be a great-great-grandson of Charles Darwin.

The more significant parallel with *Scopes* was when the supporters of intelligent design were cross-examined on the witness stand.

While the Dover trial did not involve larger-than-life, nationally known, and flamboyant personalities like the Scopes trial or climax as dramatically as when Clarence Darrow questioned William Jennings Bryan, it did have its comedic moments. The highlight was when ID theorist Michael Behe, who had advocated broadening the definition of science so that ID could be included under it, was forced to concede under cross-examination that such a broadened definition would result in even astrology being considered a science. Observers considered that moment a pivotal one in dooming ID supporters' claim to scientific status for their theory.

The fact is that religious ideas simply do not stand up well under the kind of close, narrow questioning that takes place in cross-examinations. Under those conditions, you cannot retreat to religion's refuge and evade direct and detailed questions about the consequences of your beliefs by responding with broad, sweeping generalizations. You have to answer the questions that are asked, and this can lead to the kinds of damaging concessions that Bryan made in the Scopes trial and Behe made in the Dover trial.

The Dover trial was a bad situation from the beginning for the ID people, especially the strategists at the Discovery Institute, because it took events out of their control and put them in the hands of people who did not really understand what ID was all about. The ID theorists were trying to implement a carefully crafted stealth strategy, avoiding any taint of religion. The Discovery Institute's Wedge strategy required everyone to be very discreet, carefully avoiding any mention of God or religion or anything remotely connected to them.

The Dover school board was much too clumsy in its attempts to introduce ID ideas into its curriculum. They had little patience for the subtlety of the slow, long-range plan envisaged by the Discovery Institute. They wanted God, the Bible, and prayer back in their schools, and they wanted it *now*. As a result, they left their religious fingerprints all over the policy in a way that the sophisticated strategists suspected would be fatal to their case. While ID strategists were walking on eggshells, the Dover school board members were clumping around in thick boots.

The Dover school board policy had its origins in a 6–3 vote in October 2004, when the board passed a resolution holding, "Students will be made aware of gaps/problems in Darwin's theory and of other theories of evolution including, but not limited to, intelligent design. Note: Origins of Life is not taught."

The actual policy to be implemented in January 2005 required that a statement be read to students in biology classes; it said, in part,

> Because Darwin's Theory is a theory, it continues to be tested as new evidence is discovered. The Theory is not a fact. Gaps in the Theory exist for which there is no evidence. A theory is defined as a well-tested explanation that unifies a broad range of observations.
>
> Intelligent Design is an explanation of the origin of life that differs from Darwin's view. The reference book, *Of Pandas and People*, is available for students who might be interested in gaining an understanding of what Intelligent Design actually involves.

The challenge to the Dover policy was not long in coming. In December 2004 some Dover parents led by Tammy Kitzmiller challenged the constitutionality of the school board's decision, setting the stage for the latest courtroom confrontation involving the teaching of evolution.

The lawsuit for the plaintiffs was filed by the ACLU of Pennsylvania[2] and included experienced constitutional attorneys from the firm of Pepper Hamilton and from Americans United for Separation of Church and State.

The lawyers who appeared for the Dover school board were from the Thomas More Law Center[3] (TMLC) based in Ann Arbor, Michigan, which saw itself as a kind of Christian counterweight to the ACLU. The center was created in 1999 by Thomas Monaghan, founder of the Domino's Pizza chain and financial backer of conservative Catholic causes. The center's website is very direct about its mission[4]: "Our purpose is to be the sword and shield for people of faith, providing legal representation without charge to defend and protect Christians and their religious beliefs in the public square."

The TMLC was eager to find a case with which to challenge the teaching of evolution and had urged the Dover school board to adopt its policy, offering to represent the board in court if challenged. The knowledge that free legal representation was available in case of need undoubtedly influenced board members in their decision to adopt a policy they knew would be controversial and likely disputed.

In enacting their policy, however, the religious members of the Dover school board, thinking they were doing God's work, effectively torpedoed the Discovery Institute's entire stealth strategy. By explicitly naming and introducing intelligent design into the science class, they were inviting a court challenge that would expose the idea of intelligent design itself to direct judicial review, something the Discovery Institute had carefully avoided, given the harsh treatment that creationism and "creation science" had faced when analyzed in court two decades earlier in the cases that led to *Edwards v. Aguillard*.

What was worse, the Dover school board even recommended a specific book, *Of Pandas and People*, which had a blatantly creationist pedigree. The book had been around a long time and in its earlier incarnations clearly advocated creationism. But creationism had been ruled in 1987's *Edwards v. Aguillard* to be a religious belief that had no place in public schools. After that setback, a "new" edition of the book came out that seemed to differ from the earlier versions mainly in the fact that someone had used the "search and replace" function of his or her word processor to replace all references to the word "creationism" with "intelligent design" or its derivatives.

Unfortunately for them, the replacement was so blatant that in one place in the drafts of this new edition, while seeking to replace the word "creationists" with "design proponents," they ended up with "cdesign proponentsists." This discovery added weight to the argument that "intelligent design" was simply creationism thinly repackaged, nothing more.

Recall that it was because of the *Edwards* decision that the Discovery Institute had carefully avoided any mention of creationism in its work. In fact, the entire Wedge strategy was based on tailoring a policy that avoided all the features of religion mentioned in that landmark decision and thus had some hope of passing future constitutional scrutiny. ID strategists feared that the courts would not likely be fooled by such a flimsy disguise as *Of Pandas and People*'s replacing the word "creationism" with "intelligent design" and its cognates. Even worse, it would make the two terms look synonymous.

In the end, the ID strategists were right to be concerned by this weakness since Judge John E. Jones III stated in his *Dover* ruling,

> By comparing the pre and post *Edwards* drafts of *Pandas*, three astonishing points emerge: (1) the definition for creation science in early drafts is identical to the definition of ID; (2) cognates of the word creation (creationism and creationist), which appeared approximately 150 times were deliberately and systematically replaced with the phrase ID; and (3) the changes occurred shortly after the Supreme Court held that creation science is religious and cannot be taught in public school science classes in *Edwards*. This word substitution is telling, significant,

and reveals that a purposeful change of *words* was effected without any corresponding change in *content*. (Italics in original)[5]

On hearing what the Dover school board was proposing to do, the Discovery Institute tried to discourage its members from proceeding. In a 2007 article reviewing the trial,[6] three people associated with the Discovery Institute described their associate Seth Cooper's behind-the scenes discussions with the Dover school board in which they expressed their concerns.

> Cooper learned about the Dover controversy in June of 2004 after reading a newspaper article, and he then called Dover school board member William Buckingham, and warned him that the board was courting legal trouble if it "require[d] students to learn about creationism or [attempted] to censor the teaching of the contemporary [presentation] of Darwin's theory or chemical origin of life scenarios." Cooper also emphasized that the Discovery Institute does not support *requiring* that the theory of ID be presented; instead, it recommends that schools cover scientific criticisms of Darwin's theory along with the scientific evidence supporting the theory. (Italics in original)

But they failed in their efforts to dissuade the Dover school board and the TMLC attorneys representing them from what they considered an ill-conceived policy that would likely not survive a legal challenge: "TMLC supported the Dover board not-withstanding the fact that the Discovery Institute privately communicated its strong reservations about the policy to TMLC attorneys."

The Dover board's actions thus made a hash of the ID strategy by mixing creationism, intelligent design, and opposition to Darwin into one big entangled mess. To make matters worse, the advocates of this Dover policy made no secret of the motives for their actions. They spoke openly and publicly in school board meetings and other public forums about their religious concerns about the teaching of evolution as well as their desire to combat it in some way and bring God back into the classroom.

Even leading ID advocate William Dembski ruefully noted[7] the problem raised by his supposed allies: "Unfortunately, members of the Dover school board have, through their actions, conflated ID with an apparent religious agenda. For instance, it doesn't help the ID side that William Buckingham, then a member of the Dover school board, in trying to get the Dover policy adopted, remarked:

'Two thousand years ago somebody died on the cross, can't some-body stand up for him?'"

It is not that Dembski doesn't agree with the religious sentiments expressed by Buckingham. In his copious writings, Dembski has made it abundantly clear that he seeks the overthrow of naturalism as the fundamental working principle in science and believes that the intelligent agency in intelligent design is the Christian God.[8] He and other intelligent design theorists were dismayed by the open and explicit expression of these views by members of the Dover school board because they knew it would seriously weaken their legal case.

As another example of the religious motivation behind the school board's actions that would cause problems during the trial, Buckingham raised money in churches to buy sixty copies of the creationist textbook *Of Pandas and People*, then gave the money to fellow board member Alan Bonsell's father, who then donated the books "anonymously" to the school's library to be made available as "reference" books for biology students. Later Buckingham and Bonsell both denied, under oath in their depositions, any knowledge of where the books had come from.

During the trial, this and other falsehoods were revealed in open court and clearly angered the judge, who said in his ruling, "It is ironic that several of these individuals, who so staunchly and proudly touted their religious convictions in public, would time and again lie to cover their tracks and disguise the real purpose behind the ID Policy."

As the Dover case prepared to go to trial on September 26, 2005, it became clear that the TMLC lawyers were overmatched. While they were surely earnest in their belief in the rightness of their cause, dedicated to fighting for it, religiously gung ho, and eager to do battle against evolution, they simply did not have the legal resources or expertise or the sheer numbers of people to mount the kind of research and sophisticated arguments necessary for such an important case. In addition, they faced a highly sophisticated and well-organized team of constitutional lawyers for the plaintiffs. The TMLC lawyers seemed out of their league.

As we have seen, the Dover school board's actions went contrary to the long-term strategy of the ID movement advanced by the Discovery Institute. But once the die was cast and the Dover policy had been adopted and challenged in the courts, the Discovery In-stitute was placed in a quandary. They could see that the TMLC was not fully up to the task facing them, but it was not clear to the institute what their own best course of action was. Should they completely disassociate themselves from the Dover school board deeds and distance themselves from the case as it went down to likely defeat? Or should they throw themselves fully into the fray, provide their own expert witnesses, pour their considerable financial and legal resources into the case, and hope to snatch an improbable victory?

While the latter was a better tactical option since it increased the chances of winning the case, it had the considerable strategic downside that if they lost the case despite their full participation, then the entire ID movement, not just the Dover school board, would be perceived as having been defeated, and this would have serious negative repercussions, possibly dooming their long-range plans.

It was a difficult choice, and the institute waffled. At first its representatives agreed to be part of the case and to provide expert witnesses, but that collaboration turned out to be short-lived, and they later withdrew, giving as their reason that the TMLC objected to their request that the Discovery Institute's own lawyers representing the expert witnesses they provided.

As a serious and negative consequence of the Discovery Institute's decision to withdraw their expert witnesses at the last minute, it was then too late for the TMLC to get alternative expert witnesses for their side. As a result, the plaintiffs were able to put forward their expert witnesses in science, philosophy, and theology to provide unrebutted testimony on important questions that thus became accepted as fact, seriously weakening the defense's case.

The whole episode caused bad feelings between the Discovery Institute and the TMLC that spilled out into the open, as the *Toledo Blade* reported on March 20, 2006, after the trial was over:

> In fact, when Mr. [Richard] Thompson [the head of the Thomas More Law Center] decided to defend the Dover intelligent design policy, he angered the group most associated with intelligent design: the Discovery Institute, a conservative think-tank based in Seattle.
>
> "We were incredibly frustrated by arrogance and bad legal judgment of goading the [Dover] school district to keep a policy that the main organization supporting intelligent design was opposed to," says John West, the associate director of the Discovery Institute's Center for Science and Culture.

The Thomas More Center acted "in the face of opposition from the group that actually represents most of the scientists who work on intelligent design." . . .

The Discovery Institute has never advocated the teaching of intelligent design, and told the Dover board to drop its policy, Mr. West says. It participated in the trial only reluctantly.

"We were in a bind," Mr. West says. "Our ideals were on trial even though it was a policy we didn't support."

Thompson countercharged that these were just excuses to hide the real reason, which was that the Discovery Institute people were essentially cowards without the courage of their convictions, people who talked tough but didn't put their beliefs on the line when it counted:

Mr. Thompson says the Discovery Institute's strategy is to dodge a fight as soon as one appears imminent.

"The moment there's a conflict they will back away. . . . They come up with some sort of compromise." But in Dover "they got some school board members that didn't want compromise."

This intramural battle between two groups supposedly on the same pro-IDC side did not augur well for the trial.

NOTES

1. See Chapman's article "God or Gorilla," *Harper's Magazine* (February 2006): 54–63, for entertaining insights into what was going on in that small town before and during the trial.

2. See www.aclupa.org/legal/legaldocket/intelligentdesigncase.

3. See www.thomasmore.org.

4. See vwww.thomasmore.org/qry/page.taf?id=23.

5. *Tammy Kitzmiller et al. v. Dover Area School District et al.*, 400 F. Supp. 2d 707 (M.D. Pa. 2005), case no. 04cv2688, www.pamd.uscourts.gov/kitzmiller/kitzmiller_342.pdf, 32.

6. David K. DeWolf, John G. West, and Casey Luskin, "Intelligent Design Will Survive *Kitzmiller v. Dover*," *Montana Law Review* 68 (May 4, 2007): 7–57; also available at www.discovery.org/scripts/viewDB/filesDB-download.php?command=download&id=1372.

7. William Dembski, *Life After Dover*, September 30, 2005, www.uncommondescent.com/intelligent-design/life-after-dover.

8. Barbara Forrest and Paul R. Gross, *Creationism's Trojan Horse: The Wedge of Intelligent Design* (Oxford: Oxford University Press, 2004), 283–90.

Chapter 17

The *Dover* Verdict

As almost everyone interested in this subject knows by now, on December 20, 2005, U.S. District Court Judge John E. Jones III ruled resoundingly in favor of the plaintiffs and against the Dover school board.

Not only did he rule that the Dover school board policy was unconstitutional, but he also criticized the school board's actions harshly and unsparingly, saying, "The breathtaking inanity of the Board's decision is evident when considered against the factual backdrop which has now been fully revealed through this trial. The students, parents, and teachers of the Dover Area School District deserved better than to be dragged into this legal maelstrom, with its resulting utter waste of monetary and personal resources."[1]

Judge Jones said in his ruling that all the Supreme Court precedents imply that "the Establishment Clause forbids not just the explicit teaching of religion, but any governmental action that endorses or has the primary purpose or effect of advancing religion."[2] He added that both the purpose and effect prongs of the Lemon test, as well as the reconceptualization of the effect prong as an endorsement test by Justice Sandra Day O'Connor, were applicable in determining the constitutionality of the *Dover* policy.

Jones said that the Dover school board's history and actions clearly showed that its members had religious motivations in implementing the board's policy. This made it easy for the judge to rule against the school board on the grounds that its policy had failed to meet the purpose prong of the Lemon test and was thus unconstitutional by virtue of that fact alone. In addition, he found that the policy also violated the effect prong and failed the endorsement test.

The judge went even further and also ruled on whether ID was science. The ID strategists at the Discovery Institute had desperately wanted to avoid having a judicial determination on this question, and the Discovery Institute and a group of people sympathetic to their views filed two amicus curiae ("friend of the court") briefs asking him *not* to rule on the question of the scientific status of ID.

The Discovery ID strategists wanted to have their theory considered a science because then it would have a better chance of passing the Lemon test for satisfying the Establishment Clause. They had claimed for over a decade that ID is science, and they did not want to risk having that shot down. They feared that the facts of the Dover case, with its mixing of creationism and ID, would influence the judge to view it as a religion.

But to the consternation of the Discovery Institute, the actual parties in the case, both plaintiffs and defense, asked the judge to rule on the broader and more fundamental question of whether ID was science. The plaintiffs had built their case by arguing that ID was a religion and not science, so they wanted the judge to recognize this in his ruling. And the TMLC was hoping to get a ruling saying that ID is science and could therefore be taught in public schools. So both sides asked for this question to be addressed, but for very different reasons.

The judge felt that determining whether ID was a science or religion was proper and justified his decision to do so by saying that the lengthy discussion on this very question during the trial meant that the issue had received a thorough airing; thus, making such a determination was both useful and even essential. He also seemed to have a more sophisticated understanding of the nature of science than Judge William R. Overton in the 1982 case of *McLean v. Arkansas Board of Education*.

Jones said, "We will offer our conclusion on whether ID is science not just because it is essential to our holding that an Establishment Clause violation has occurred in this case, but also in the hope that it may prevent the obvious waste of judicial and other resources which would be occasioned by a subsequent trial involving the precise question which is before us."[3]

He then ruled that based on the testimony presented in the case, ID is not science but a religion. His full opinion on how he came to this conclusion is well worth reading because it gives an excellent summary of some basic ideas in the history, philosophy, and methodology of science.

His reasoning on this point is also likely to be influential because, although, like the Scopes trial, this case will not reach the Supreme Court, this topic received such an exhaustive examination during the trial and his opinion analyzed it in such detail that it seems likely to cast a similarly long shadow. Any future case involving intelligent design will depend heavily on his opinion and thus have a strong presumption that ID is a religion and not science.

Appeals courts, especially the U.S. Supreme Court, are not well suited to get into adjudicating the facts of a case. Furthermore, oral arguments before appeals courts usually last less than an hour and sometimes are not even presented. Hence, appeals courts tend to defer on issues of fact to determinations made by lower courts.

This is what happened with the U.S. Supreme Court in the 1987 case of *Edwards v. Aguillard*, in which the Court depended heavily on the analysis of the nature of creation science written by U.S. District Judge Overton in the 1982 case of *McLean v. Arkansas Board of Education*. Hence, Judge Jones's ruling that ID is not a science but a religion is likely to be extremely damaging to ID's future prospects.

Judge Jones said in his ruling,[4]

> After a searching review of the record and applicable case law, we find that while ID arguments may be true, a proposition on which the Court takes no position, ID is not science. We find that ID fails on three different levels, any one of which is sufficient to preclude a determination that ID is science. They are: (1) ID violates the centuries-old ground rules of science by invoking and permitting supernatural causation; (2) the argument of irreducible complexity, central to ID, employs the same flawed and illogical contrived dualism that doomed creation science in the 1980s; and (3) ID's negative attacks on evolution have been refuted by the scientific community. As we will discuss in more detail below, it is additionally important to note that ID has failed to gain acceptance in the scientific community, it has not generated peer-reviewed publications, nor has it been the subject of testing and research.

He added, "It is notable that not one defense expert was able to explain how the supernatural action suggested by ID could be anything other than an inherently religious proposition."[5] He also pointed to the expert evidence given by the pro-ID witnesses themselves (Michael Behe, Scott Minnich, and Steven Fuller), to statements made elsewhere by other leading ID figures like Phillip Johnson and William Dembski, and to the *Edwards* and *McLean* precedents to conclude that "ID's religious nature is evident because it involves a supernatural designer."[6]

We saw that the history of the words and actions of some Dover school board members had made it fairly easy to determine that the board had violated the purpose prong of the Lemon test. To determine whether it had also violated the effect prong and the endorsement test (as articulated in *Lynch*), Judge Jones said in his ruling that what determines whether a law passes constitutional muster on these grounds is not only how one parses the actual wording of the legislation but also whether a *reasonable and informed observer* (as defined in Justice O'Connor's concurring opinion in *Elk Grove*) would interpret the effect of the law as an endorsement of a particular religious viewpoint.

Judge Jones said that in general "the test consists of the reviewing court determining what message a challenged governmental policy or enactment conveys to a reasonable, objective observer *who knows the policy's language, origins, and legislative history, as well as the history of the community and the broader social and historical context in which the policy arose*" (my italics).[7]

On the specific issue of challenges to evolutionary theory, he looked at history and legal precedent and especially at "a factor that weighed heavily in the Supreme Court's decision to strike down the balanced-treatment law in *Edwards*, specifically that '[o]ut of many possible science subjects taught in the public schools, the legislature chose to affect the teaching of the one scientific theory that historically has been opposed by certain religious sects.'"[8]

He concluded, "In singling out the one scientific theory that has historically been opposed by certain religious sects, the Board sent the message that it 'believes there is some problem peculiar to evolution,' and '[i]n light of the historical opposition to evolution by Christian fundamentalists and creationists[,]. . . *the informed, reasonable observer would infer the School Board's problem with evolution to be that evolution does not acknowledge a creator*'" (my italics).[9]

When they crafted their strategy back in 1993, ID advocates could not have anticipated Justice O'Connor's introduction in 2004's Elk Grove case of the "informed, reasonable observer" as the standard for judging the purpose of the law under the Establishment Clause.

ID advocates and supporters had tried to implement their plan by carefully choosing words and sentences free of any obviously religious connotations so that they would meet the *letter* of the law, hoping that the policy would thereby pass constitutional scrutiny. But Judge Jones said that it is not merely how the law is worded but also how a particular kind of observer, *who is assumed to be much more knowledgeable about the issues than your average person in the street*, would interpret the intent of the law.

This is where the ghost of the Scopes trial appears again. Ever since that trial, the presumption has been that anyone who opposes the theory of evolution has primarily religious reasons for doing so.[10] Justice Antonin Scalia, in his dissent in *Edwards*,[11] acknowledged the existence of "an intellectual predisposition created by the facts and the legend of *Scopes* . . . an instinctive reaction that any governmentally imposed requirements bearing upon the teaching of evolution must be a manifestation of Christian fundamentalist repression." As a result, the burden of proof is now on those who oppose evolution to prove that they do not have religious reasons for doing so, and that is a high standard to meet.

In a further telling statement that has direct implications for the Discovery Institute's "teach the controversy" strategy, Judge Jones said, "ID's backers have sought to avoid the scientific scrutiny which we have now determined that it cannot withstand by advocating that the controversy, but not ID itself, should be taught in science class. This tactic is at best disingenuous, and at worst a canard. The goal of the IDM [intelligent design movement] is not to encourage critical thought, but to foment a revolution which would supplant evolutionary theory with ID."[12]

In other words, he had seen right through the entire Wedge strategy.

This is a very damaging part of the verdict for the ID case. ID strategy has always been to undermine the credibility of evolutionary theory in science by singling it out for special scrutiny. After all, ID proponents have not been calling for "critical analysis" and "teaching the controversy" in *all* areas of science. Judge Jones said that since an "informed, reasonable observer" would know that Christians have had long-standing objections to evolutionary theory on religious grounds, such an observer would see singling it out for adversarial treatment as tantamount to endorsing a religious viewpoint.

There is no way to see the *Dover* ruling as anything but a devastating blow to the entire stealth strategy promoted by the Discovery Institute. It took apart every element of their carefully constructed edifice, leaving only rubble.

Just after the trial ended on November 4, 2005, but before the judge delivered his verdict, the Dover school board elections were held, and a slate of anti-ID candidates, including one of the plaintiffs, was elected, replacing all eight of the former pro-ID people up for reelection. As a result, the *Dover* verdict will not be appealed to a higher court and thus, like the Scopes trial, will not formally set a legal precedent for the nation.

Nonetheless, although the *Dover* decision is not legally binding on any court outside the jurisdiction of the district court, *Dover*'s legal impact will be far ranging. This is because the *Kitzmiller* decision, unlike that in *Scopes*, actually addressed the scientific and constitutional issues in an exhaustive manner and thus provides legal guidance that other courts faced with similar cases might well find persuasive.

NOTES

1. *Tammy Kitzmiller et al. v. Dover Area School District et al.*, 400 F. Supp. 2d 707 (M. D. Pa. 2005), case no. 04cv2688, www.pamd.uscourts.gov/kitzmiller/kitzmiller_342.pdf, 138.

2. *Kitzmiller v. Dover Area School District*, 46.

3. *Kitzmiller v. Dover Area School District*, 63.

4. *Kitzmiller v. Dover Area School District*, 64.

5. *Kitzmiller v. Dover Area School District*, 31.

6. *Kitzmiller v. Dover Area School District*, 29.

7. *Kitzmiller v. Dover Area School District*, 15.

8. *Kitzmiller v. Dover Area School District*, 48.

9. *Kitzmiller v. Dover Area School District*, 57.

10. I have noticed this personally. When people tell me they are skeptical about the theory of evolution, they often quickly add that their opposition is not due to religious reasons.

11. *Edwards v. Aguillard*, 482 U.S. 578, www.law.cornell.edu/supct/html/historics/USSC_CR_0482_0578_ZD.html.

12. *Kitzmiller v. Dover Area School District*, 89.

Chapter 18

The Aftershocks of *Dover*

The implications of the *Dover* verdict were felt almost immediately. The decision reverberated across the nation, the sweep of it knocking down one pro-ID policy after another like a row of dominoes.

On January 17, 2006, in a school in El Tejon, California, a new elective philosophy course that included intelligent design ideas was abruptly canceled out of concern that it, too, would be ruled unconstitutional. The Discovery Institute, reeling from the battering its ideas had received in *Dover*, pressured the school district to take this action, concerned that this was another misguided policy by a local school board that would hurt ID even more.

In February 2006, Ohio's State Board of Education reversed its previous policy and ruled 11–4 to throw out its ID-inspired science standards benchmarks calling for "critical analysis" of evolution, the majority saying that the *Dover* verdict meant that such a policy, if challenged, would also be ruled unconstitutional. State school board elections later that year resulted in the most vocal ID supporter resoundingly losing her seat on the board, getting less than 30 percent of the vote.

What happened in Kansas is also telling. During 2005, riding the crest of a pro-ID wave, the Kansas State Board of Education, in the teeth of opposition from scientists locally and nationwide, decided to adopt science standards laced with pro-ID language; they deliberately undermined the credibility of the theory of evolution and went so far as to broaden the definition of science to allow for nonmaterial causes for phenomena so that ID ideas could be included as science.[1]

These new standards were adopted on November 8, 2005, after the Dover trial had ended but before the verdict was handed down.

In primary elections held in August 2006 following the verdict, however, the pro-ID faction on Kansas's school board lost its majority, and in the November 2006 general election, those who favored science over ID obtained a narrow 6–4 majority. As a result, on February 13, 2007, the new state board of education reversed itself[2] and replaced the old standards with new ones that eliminated the earlier ID-inspired criticisms of evolutionary theory. The revised standards also required methodological naturalism to be the underlying basis of scientific investigations, thus eliminating nonmaterial causes as explanations for physical phenomena.

But Kansas has seesawed on this issue based on school board election results since 1999, so the story there may not be over, even though the standards are not *required* to be revised again until 2014.

The El Tejon case mentioned above, although it never went to court, is a good example of the problem that advocates of religion in schools face. After all, in El Tejon they claimed they were merely seeking to teach ID ideas as part of a purely elective philosophy course, not as science. The initiators of the course felt that surely this should be allowable. But the course description should have put on the alert anyone familiar with the legislative history of the Establishment Clause.

The document said,

Philosophy of Intelligent Design: This class will take a close look at evolution as a theory and will discuss the scientific, biological, and Biblical aspects that suggest why Darwin's philosophy is not rock solid. This class will discuss Intelligent Design as an alternative response to evolution. Topics that will be covered are the age of the earth, a world wide flood, dinosaurs, pre-human fossils, dating methods, DNA, radioisotopes, and geological evidence. Physical and chemical evidence will be presented suggesting the earth is thousands of years old, not billions. The class will include lecture discussions, guest speakers, and videos. The class grade will be based on a position paper in which students will support or refute the theory of evolution.

The problem with this course is that, as Judge John E. Jones III pointed out in the Dover case, all applicable Supreme Court precedents imply that "the Establishment Clause forbids not just the explicit teaching of religion, but any governmental action that endorses or has the primary purpose or effect of advancing religion."³ And the El Tejon course clearly does endorse it.

Furthermore, Judge Jones said in his ruling, "Our conclusion today is that it is unconstitutional to teach ID *as an alternative to evolution* in a public school classroom"⁴ (my italics), and the El Tejon course tries to do just that.

But that leaves open the question of whether ID can be taught at all in public schools, as long as it is not contrasted with evolution.

The law and the precedents seem to indicate that there would be no problem under these guidelines about a course that examined, *in a neutral way*, the religious beliefs of people. There would be no problem in discussing in a history or social studies or philosophy course the role that Christianity played in the American political process or the role that Islam played in the development of the Middle East or the way that religious beliefs have influenced philosophical thought. In fact, it would be hard to keep religion out and still teach those topics in a meaningful way.

As Justice Thomas Clark wrote in his majority opinion⁵ in *Abington v. Schempp*, "It might well be said that one's education is not complete without a study of comparative religion or the history of religion and its relationship to the advancement of civilization. It certainly may be said that the Bible is worthy of study for its literary and historic qualities. Nothing we have said here indicates that such study of the Bible or of religion, *when presented objectively as part of a secular program of education*, may not be effected consistently with the First Amendment" (my italics).

A problem only arises if you use a course to *promote* religion in general or a specific religious point of view.

Now we can see more clearly why the El Tejon course was problematic. It is not how a course is labeled (whether as science or philosophy or history or whatever) that is at issue; it is the *purpose* of the course and whether it would seem, to an *informed, reasonable observer* who is *familiar with the history and context* of the issue at hand, to *endorse* a particular religious viewpoint. The El Tejon course was clearly advocating young-Earth creationism, and the people at the Discovery Institute (rightly, I think) saw that this would easily be ruled unconstitutional. Since the course, like in *Dover*, explicitly dragged in intelligent design by name, another negative ruling in this case would be interpreted as meaning that ID ideas should not be allowed even in philosophy classes, which would be a huge public relations setback for proponents. In addition, they would likely have been disturbed by the El Tejon school board implying that intelligent design belonged in a philosophy course, since their entire strategy all along has been to argue that it is science.

Where does this leave the question of teaching evolution in schools? The *Dover* verdict seems to have closed the last small window that remained for inserting ID ideas into the science curriculum. This setback has led to a feeling of discouragement in the ID camp. Leading Wedge strategist and founder of the ID movement Phillip Johnson sounded like he was throwing in the towel in an interview[6] he gave in 2006.

He essentially conceded that the ID people had failed to deliver the goods when it came to providing the kinds of evidence and arguments necessary for ID to even be considered as science, let along succeed in science. It is precisely that combination of evidence and persuasive arguments that had made Darwinian evolutionary theory such a scientific powerhouse, comparable in its impact and scope to Newton's and Einstein's theories.

Johnson said,

> I considered [Dover] a loser from the start. . . . Where you have a board writing a statement and telling the teachers to repeat it to the class, I thought that was a very bad idea. . . .
>
> *I also don't think that there is really a theory of intelligent design at the present time to propose as a comparable alternative to the Darwinian theory, which is, whatever errors it might contain, a fully worked out scheme. There is no intelligent design theory that's comparable.* Working out a positive theory is the job of the scientific people that we have affiliated with the movement. Some of them are quite convinced that it's doable, but that's for them to prove. . . . *No product is ready for competition in the educational world.* . . .
>
> I think the fat lady has sung for any efforts to change the approach in the public schools. . . . The courts are just not going to allow it. They never have. The efforts to change things in the public schools generate more powerful opposition than accomplish anything. . . . I don't think that means the end of the issue at all. . . .
>
> In some respects, I'm almost relieved, and glad. *I think the issue is properly settled.* It's clear to me now that the public schools are not going to change their line in my lifetime. (My italics)

But Johnson, even though one of its founders and intellectual leaders, may not be speaking for the ID movement anymore. Some of ID's followers are still seeking ways to make it viable again.

NOTES

1. I was involved in a minor way in that controversy, being one of the scientists invited to take part in hearings. The scientific community concluded that these were sham hearings and called for a boycott, and I did not testify.

2. Associated Press, Kansas board boosts evolution education, February 14, 2007, www.msnbc.msn.com/id/17132925.

3. *Tammy Kitzmiller et al. v. Dover Area School District et al.*, 400 F. Supp. 2d 707 (M.D. Pa. 2005), case no. 04cv2688, www.pamd.uscourts.gov/kitzmiller/kitzmiller_342.pdf, 46.

4. *Kitzmiller v. Dover Area School District*, 137.

5. *School District of Abington Township, Pennsylvania v. Schempp*, 374 U.S. 203, www.law.cornell.edu/supct/html/historics/USSC_CR_0374_0203_ZO.html.

6. Michelangelo D'Agostino, "In the Matter of *Berkeley v. Berkeley*," *Berkeley Science Review* (spring 2006): 31, http://sciencereview.berkeley.edu/articles/issue10/evolution.pdf.

Chapter 19

What Next?

The long string of judicial rulings and Supreme Court precedents seem to have eliminated almost all the options for religious people to combat the teaching of evolution in public schools. But they are still trying. There are rumblings that Texas may try to get creationism and/or intelligent design creationism and/or criticisms of evolution into its state curriculum. The state's science curriculum director was forced to resign her position,[1] and some suspect that this was a prelude to making such changes. It is hard to see how Texas can be successful in such efforts given the weight of prior judicial verdicts on this issue.

There seem to be only four options left for those trying to find something, anything, with which to undermine the teaching of evolution or otherwise get religion back into the public schools.

One option (suggested in Ohio in 2006 but then quickly abandoned) is not to single out just evolution for "critical analysis" but to include a few other theories as well and use them as a cover for the real goal of discrediting evolution. But given the legislative history of opposition to teaching evolution in schools, the courts will likely see through this as merely yet another ruse to circumvent the Establishment Clause and understand that the real purpose of such policies is once again to single out "the one scientific theory that has historically been opposed by certain religious sects." That alone makes such policies constitutionally suspect.

Another option is to ask that *all* scientific theories be subjected to critical analysis. This might pass constitutional muster but would not serve the purpose that religious people seek. It is, after all, what good science teaching has always professed to do and is already routinely called for in present-day science standards.

While it may be possible to formulate camouflaging language and policies in such a way that the religious motivations for opposing the teaching of evolution are buried deeply enough to pass constitutional scrutiny, such a watered-down version will essentially result in what has always existed: individual teachers will be able to sneak creationist ideas and sentiment into their teaching in an ad hoc way. To significantly undermine the teaching of evolution, school districts will have to use lesson plans designed along these lines, and such official and targeted actions against evolution are unlikely to pass the Lemon or endorsement tests.

The problem for religious people is that they have no concerns about, for example, the theory of gravity or Newton's laws of motion or the heliocentric model of the solar system or the laws of photosynthesis, and presumably they don't want their children's time wasted on discussing evidence against those theories or speculating on why they too might be wrong and the associated processes driven by an intelligent designer. What really bothers religious people is the theory of evolution, so not specifically targeting it in some way does not serve their purposes.

A third, fairly extreme option advocated by some religious groups is to try to undermine and destroy the public school system entirely, leaving parents only with private, parochial, or homeschooling options, all of which are outside the reach of the Establishment Clause protections.

The final option is to seek what ID advocate Phillip Johnson seemed to be hinting at in his interview discussed in the previous chapter—to arouse public opinion against evolution theory in order to foment some type of popular revolution against it.

It is not clear what is hoped for here. As I see it, ID proponents can only succeed along these lines by calling for the overthrow of the Establishment Clause and undermining the whole idea of separation of church and state. But this is a huge barrier to overcome.

The Bill of Rights in the U.S. Constitution has come to be seen as providing the bedrock freedoms of American society. Over time, these protections have been expanded but never formally restricted, although various presidential administrations and Congresses have occasionally curtailed those freedoms in times of emergency. Despite such temporary setbacks for basic liberties and justice, it seems unlikely that any attempt to formally rescind or restrict those constitutional freedoms will succeed.

Those who seek to undermine the Establishment Clause because it prohibits the insertion of their particular religious beliefs into public schools, courthouses, government, and other agencies of the state would do well to heed Justice Sandra Day O'Connor's warning in her concurring opinion in a 2005 case ruling the display of the Ten Commandments in courthouses to be a violation of the Establishment Clause. She wrote,[2]

> Reasonable minds can disagree about how to apply the Religion Clauses in a given case. But the goal of the Clauses is clear: to carry out the Founders' plan of preserving religious liberty to the fullest extent possible in a pluralistic society. By enforcing the Clauses, we have kept religion a matter for the individual conscience, not for the prosecutor or bureaucrat. At a time when we see around the world the violent consequences of the assumption of religious authority by government, Americans may count themselves fortunate: Our regard for constitutional boundaries has protected us from similar travails, while allowing private religious exercise to flourish. . . . Those who would renegotiate the boundaries between church and state must therefore answer a difficult question: Why would we trade a system that has served us so well for one that has served others so poorly?

Whatever the long-term goal, the immediate response of ID followers to the *Dover* verdict was to try to discredit it, arguing that it was due to "judicial activism" and overreaching by a biased judge with ambitions to greatness. In 2006 the Discovery Institute published a book called *Traipsing into Evolution*[3] attacking the judge's verdict and reasoning.

The charge that Judge John E. Jones III, who presided in the Dover trial, is some kind of antireligious political partisan is hard to sustain. As we have seen, the judge's verdict was strongly constrained by prior judicial rulings. Furthermore, a Republican and long-time member of a Lutheran church, the judge was sponsored for his post by then U.S. Senator Rick Santorum (himself a strong supporter of intelligent design) and was nominated to the bench by then-President George W. Bush (who has argued that "both sides" of the evolution issue, whatever that means, should be taught). His assignment to the Dover case was praised by Tom Ridge (former Republican governor of Pennsylvania and then head of the Department of Homeland

Security), who said, "I can't imagine a better judge presiding over such an emotionally charged issue."

The judge himself seemed to anticipate this kind of attack and preemptively responded to it in his opinion, saying,

> Those who disagree with this ruling will likely mark it as the product of an activist judge. If so, they will have erred as this is manifestly not an activist court. Rather, this case came to us as the result of the activism of an ill-informed faction on a school board, aided by a national public interest law firm eager to find a constitutional test case on ID, who in combination drove the Board to adopt an imprudent and ultimately unconstitutional policy. The breathtaking inanity of the Board's decision is evident when considered against the factual backdrop which has now been fully revealed through this trial.[4]

On another front, in 2007, ID advocate Michael Behe published another book trying to resurrect the idea of intelligent design.[5] According to a review[6] by Jerry Coyne (professor of ecology and evolution at the University of Chicago), the only "new" idea in this book compared to his previous effort is to argue that the mutations that drive natural selection are not random but are somehow *guided* by their peripatetic and secretive designer to achieve a desired organism.[7]

This feeble attempt is unlikely to get anywhere legally. All the reasons given in the *Dover* verdict for why ID is a religion and not science apply with equal force to this idea too. Furthermore, it is not even an original idea, having been proposed in the late nineteenth century by eminent scientists Asa Gray, Charles Lyell, St. George Mivart, and Richard Owen[8] soon after Charles Darwin published *On the Origin of Species* in 1859. Those earlier scientists also had manifestly religious reasons for making their suggestion, a fact that is not going to help the ID case legally.

There is also a film called *Expelled: No Intelligence Allowed*, released on Darwin's birthday in 2008,[9] which argues that "big science" is deliberately suppressing evidence of intelligent design and persecuting scientists who think there is something in it.[10]

The film seemingly aims to portray ID advocates as victims, oppressed by the scientific and legal establishment. It advances the strange argument that scientists are secretly aware of terrible weaknesses in evolutionary theory but fear that the revolutionary new arguments of the courageous ID advocates will result in the structure of science crumbling. Scientists can only prevent this, in their view, by colluding to cover up the facts, suppressing all dissent, and expelling pro-ID people from the academy.

This truly bizarre argument betrays a deep lack of awareness of how science works. The goal of any scientist, one that guarantees immense prestige and recognition, is to overthrow a well-established scientific theory and create a scientific revolution. The names of Copernicus, Newton, Darwin, and Einstein are testaments to the lasting fame that accompanies successful efforts to overthrow estab-

What Might Darwin have Thought about the Turmoil His Work Aroused across the Atlantic?

Charles Darwin was by no means possessed of a revolutionary spirit. He was very much an establishment figure, shy and retiring in manner, avoiding crowds and the social life, happiest when left alone in his country home with his family, his work, and his correspondence. He can best be described as a reluctant revolutionary, who knew that his work would cause a major upheaval in society. He was hesitant to trigger the turmoil by publishing his theory, doing so only when he was about to be scooped by Alfred Russell Wallace.

At the same time, Darwin was intensely proud of his groundbreaking theory and convinced of its rightness based on the evidence to hand, although he was well aware of the major gaps in his argument and the data, many of which had to wait for a century of research before being filled in.

I think he would have been pleased to view the controversy in America from a distance across the ocean and would have followed it closely in the media but avoided any personal involvement. He would have enjoyed seeing his work become the standard biological model and the scientific community rising to defend his theory and pouring so much energy into combating those who would deny its truth.

lished theories. The idea that there are scientists out there who have convincing evidence that the theory of evolution is false but are sitting on it out of a desire to protect "big science" is preposterous.

In reality, scientists do not embrace ideas like ID because they are confident of the merits of the theory of evolution even though they know it has not answered every question as yet. They reject ID because it is an old idea with no content of any value or use to scientists. Its use of supernatural explanations robs it of all predictive power, and predictions lie at the heart of the entire scientific enterprise. Scientists are always looking for things they predict they should see.

But even if the film's strategy of painting ID followers as the somewhat pitiful and oppressed victims of the scientific establishment succeeds and arouses some public sympathy, I cannot see any way for this strategy to achieve the goal of overthrowing the teaching of evolution in schools, since all previous attempts to do so have run aground on the rocks of the Establishment Clause of the First Amendment to the U.S. Constitution.

But constitutional issues aside, the important question has always been about who determines what should and should not be taught in public schools. "Who does have 'the right,' [Yale law professor Stephen L. Carter] asked, to decide what gets taught as science in the public schools? Creationist parents and teachers, based on their relatively subjective religious beliefs, or professional scientists and educators, based on their relatively objective scientific theories?"[11] This is an interesting question to explore.

As we saw in the 1982 *McLean v. Arkansas Board of Education* creation science case, the judge ruled that creation science should not be taught because it is not science but a religion. Some supporters of that decision criticized the reasoning that led to it, saying that the reason creation science should not be taught was not because it had failed to meet what they considered unjustifiable demarcation criteria but because it was bad science and simply wrong.

But is the teaching of even manifestly absurd ideas a sufficient reason for the courts to intervene? If a school district decides that it should teach something absurd or even flat-out wrong, for instance, that the moon is made of cheese, is it allowed to do so? Can a parent complain and have the courts overturn such a policy? What would be the constitutional basis for such an action?

In 1926, in oral arguments during the appeal of the *Scopes* verdict to the Tennessee Supreme Court, defense counsel Arthur Garfield Hays raised the interesting possibility that the Fourteenth Amendment to the U.S. Constitution prevented the state from enforcing *unreasonable* laws and that "Tennessee's 'absurd' antievolution statute violated this standard as much as a law against teaching Copernican astronomy would."[12] But as far as I know, this issue of the constitutionality of teaching patently absurd ideas in public schools has not been adjudicated.

Although this is an interesting hypothetical exercise, in reality we may never be able to disentangle the ridiculous from the religious. Only when religious convictions drive their beliefs, for instance, that the Earth is six thousand years old or that God intervened in the laws of nature to create humans, do people feel strongly enough about teaching things for which there is no evidence to appeal to the courts or legislatures to intervene and enforce such policies.

Meanwhile, there is no unity among those supporters of evolutionary theory who oppose the teaching of creationism and its derivatives, like intelligent design, in public schools. These divisions arise because of differences in attitudes toward religion.

On the one hand, there are those (both religious and nonreligious people) who think that although mainstream religious beliefs are credible and valuable, it is a good idea to keep church and state separate.

There are those who feel that while religious beliefs are *not* credible, political alliances need to be made with those religious people who do not seek to insert religion into the public sphere (in public schools and elsewhere) and thus are willing to mute their view that religious beliefs are fundamentally irrational.

These two groups join forces to argue on narrow constitutional Establishment Clause grounds that religious beliefs do not belong in public schools.

But there is a growing third group, those who are more sympathetic to Clarence Darrow's approach in the Scopes trial. He seemed to have a different goal. He set out to argue that religious beliefs were nonsense and that no sensible person should believe them, let alone want to teach them to their children. After all, no one is asking schools to teach children other nonsensical ideas such as that the Earth is flat, that the Sun orbits the Earth, or that there are fairies at the bottom of the garden. No legal steps have been necessary (at least not yet) to prevent teachers from telling students that thunder and lightning are symbols of God's anger with the world or that objects fall to the ground because the Earth is at the center of the universe.

When Darrow said in his interrogation of William Jennings Bryan, "You insult every man of science and learning in the world because he does not believe in your fool religion," he was trying to make a different point: if you can show that a belief is silly, then no one will even *want* to teach that belief. And he felt that religious beliefs were patently ridiculous, requiring people to swallow, without any evidence, the most preposterous of ideas.

As Larson says, "Darrow . . . used his defense of Scopes to challenge fundamentalist beliefs. To the extent that lawyers defending the evolutionist position in later lawsuits appeal narrowly to constitutional interpretation, fundamentalist beliefs remain unchallenged."[13]

Darrow's basic approach has been extended by the so-called new atheists. These are modern-day scientists and atheists like Richard Dawkins,[14] Sam Harris,[15] and Victor Stenger[16] who argue that even "moderate" religious beliefs are absurd and one should not pretend that the beliefs of mainstream religions have any credibility just to achieve short-term tactical and legal victories. Scientific knowledge is fundamentally incompatible with the supernatural ideas of religion, and there is no intellectually honest way of reconciling the two.

They contend that "moderate" religious beliefs and "fundamentalist" religious beliefs are two sides of the same coin and that one cannot argue against the latter without ultimately seeking to eliminate the former as well. They deny any claim by so-called mainstream religious beliefs to immunity from criticism.

In taking this approach, they provide yet another echo from the Scopes trial era. Writer H. L. Mencken took a similar stand when he wrote in defense of Clarence Darrow's performance in the Scopes trial against those who felt that his questioning of Bryan was effectively targeting all religion, not just the beliefs of antievolution fundamentalists. It is worth quoting Mencken at length.[17]

The meaning of religious freedom, I fear, is sometimes greatly misapprehended. It is taken to be a sort of immunity, not merely from governmental control but also from public opinion. A dunderhead gets himself a long-tailed coat, rises behind the sacred desk, and emits such bilge as would gag a Hottentot. Is it to pass unchallenged? If so, then what we have is not religious freedom at all, but the most intolerable and outrageous variety of religious despotism. Any fool, once he is admitted to holy orders, becomes infallible. Any half-wit, by the simple device of ascribing his delusions to revelation, takes on an authority that is denied to all the rest of us.

I do not know how many Americans entertain the ideas defended so ineptly by poor Bryan, but probably the number is very large. They are preached once a week in at least a hundred thousand rural churches, and they are heard too in the meaner quarters of the great cities. Nevertheless, though they are thus held to be sound by millions, these ideas remain mere rubbish. Not only are they not supported by the known facts; they are in direct contravention of the known facts. No man whose information is sound and whose mind functions normally can conceivably credit them. They are the products of ignorance and stupidity, either or both.

What should be a civilized man's attitude toward such superstitions? It seems to me that the only attitude possible to him is one of contempt. If he admits that they have any intellectual dignity whatever, he admits that he himself has none. If he pretends to a respect for those who believe in them, he pretends falsely, and sinks almost to their level. When he is challenged he must answer honestly, regardless of tender feelings. That is what Darrow did at Dayton, and the issue plainly justified the act. Bryan went there in a hero's shining armor, bent deliberately upon a gross crime against sense. He came out a wrecked and preposterous charlatan, his tail between his legs. Few Americans have ever done so much for their country in a whole lifetime as Darrow did in two hours.

As I have said above, not all those who think religious beliefs have no foundation support this approach. Other groups prefer to take a more accommodating stand toward what is known as mainstream religion.

The intramural struggle among groups that support the teaching of evolution goes on, just like the one among those who oppose it.

NOTES

1. Terrence Stutz, *Former state science director sues over intelligent design e-mail*, The Dallas Morning News, July 3, 2008, http://www.dallasnews.com/sharedcontent/dws/dn/education/stories/070408dntexscience.184e885c.html.

2. *McCreary County, Kentucky, et al., Petitioners, v. American Civil Liberties Union of Kentucky et al.* 545 U.S. 844 No. 03-1693, www.law.cornell.edu/supct/html/03-1693.ZC.html.

3. David K. Dewolf, John G. West, Casey Luskin, and Jonathan Witt, *Traipsing into Evolution* (Seattle, WA: Discovery Institute, 2006). For a detailed critique of this book, see www.ncseweb.org/resources/rncse_content/vol26/3984_itraipsing_into_evolution_i_12_30_1899.asp.

4. *Tammy Kitzmiller et al. v. Dover Area School District et al.*, 400 F. Supp. 2d 707 (M.D. Pa. 2005), case no. 04cv2688, www.pamd.uscourts.gov/kitzmiller/kitzmiller_342.pdf, 138.

5. Michael Behe, *The Edge of Evolution: The Search for the Limits to Darwinism* (New York: Free Press, 2007).

6. Jerry Coyne, *The Great Mutator*, Talk Reason, June 14, 2007, www.talkreason.org/articles/Mutator.cfm.

7. For an even more detailed review of Behe's book, see Paul R. Gross, "Design for Living," *New Criterion* (October 2007), www.creationismstrojanhorse.com/Gross_Behe_Review_10.2007.pdf.

8. Adrian Desmond and James Moore, *Darwin: The Life of a Tortured Evolutionist* (New York: W. W. Norton & Company, 1991), 545.

9. Dan Whipple of *Colorado Confidential* got to see a preview of the film, and you can read his review at www.coloradoconfidential.com/showDiary.do?diaryId=3229.

10. Cornelia Dean, "Scientists Feel Miscast in Film on Life's Origin," *New York Times*, September 27, 2007, www.nytimes.com/2007/09/27/science/27expelled.html?hp.

11. Edward J. Larson, *Summer for the Gods* (Cambridge, MA: Harvard University Press, 1997), 260.

12. Larson, *Summer for the Gods*, 215.

13. Larson, *Summer for the Gods*, 261.

14. Richard Dawkins, *The God Delusion* (Boston: Houghton Mifflin, 2006).

15. Sam Harris, *Letter to a Christian Nation* (New York: Knopf, 2006) and *The End of Faith* (New York: W. W. Norton & Company, 2004).

16. Victor Stenger, *God: The Failed Hypothesis* (Amherst, NY: Prometheus Books, 2007).

17. H.L.Mencken,"Bryan," *Baltimore Evening Sun*, September 14, 1925, www.positiveatheism.org/hist/menck05.htm#SCOPESC.

Chapter 20

The Long View

It might be helpful to step back and look at the big picture, to see both *how* the struggle to oppose the teaching of evolution evolved as a result of legal decisions based on the First Amendment and *why* religious believers have pursued with such vigor this policy to discredit evolution, which has repeatedly led them to dead ends.

Religious people have always been uncomfortable with the theory of evolution. The extent of this discomfort varies depending on where one stands in the spectrum of religious beliefs.

At one end of this religious spectrum, we have those biblical literalists who want to believe that every single existing species was created specially by God. For these people, almost every aspect of the theory of evolution is anathema.

Somewhere in the middle of the spectrum are those willing to accept an interconnected and evolving tree of life, provided that humans are not part of the tree and were somehow miraculously created separately. Such people accept the theory of evolution as the explanation in some areas but arbitrarily exclude it from any involvement in the origins of humans.

At the other end of the religious spectrum are those who accept that humans are also part of the evolutionary tree and have common ancestors with other species but want to reserve some special property of humans (the "soul" for want of a better word) that is created by God using some mysterious means beyond our understanding. Such people want to believe that each human being possesses something special, unique, and mystical whose creation and existence cannot be accounted for by the mechanisms of natural selection.

All these people fear that lurking in the shadows of Darwinian theory is the fact that if you carry the theory of evolution to
its logical conclusion, there is absolutely no way of avoiding the
recognition that humans, like every other species of living thing,
are *entirely* the product of the Darwinian mutation and natural selection algorithmic process; thus, they are entirely material objects
produced by materialistic mechanisms. God is ruled completely out
of the picture.

William Jennings Bryan correctly understood this implication
way back in 1922, when he wrote in his *New York Times* essay, "If a
man accepts Darwinism, or evolution applied to man, *and is consistent*, he rejects the miracle and the supernatural as impossible. . . .
Evolution naturally leads to agnosticism and, if continued, finally to
atheism" (my italics).

So, while the form and tactics of the fight against the teaching of evolution have undoubtedly changed since the time of William Jennings
Bryan and the Scopes trial, the one constant feature underlying that
struggle has been the feeling that the theory of evolution is somehow
dangerous to religion and either it must be overthrown or arbitrarily
limited in its scope or its teaching balanced with ideas favorable to a
God-centered view of life and creation. But all efforts so far to limit the
scope of teaching "Darwin's dangerous idea" (as Daniel Dennett puts
it[1]) in public schools have run headlong into the wall of the Establishment Clause of the First Amendment to the U.S. Constitution and its
associated idea of the separation of church and state.

The Establishment Clause, which consists of the simple and terse
statement "Congress shall make no law respecting an establishment
of religion" has over time been fleshed out under successive court
rulings to mean that all bodies acting as agents of federal, state, or
local governments are expected to act strictly neutrally between religions and between religion and nonreligion. To pass muster, their
policies should have a secular purpose, should not have the primary
effect of advancing or inhibiting religion, should not excessively en-
tangle the government with religion, and should not, when viewed
by an informed, reasonable observer who is familiar with the history and context of the issue at hand, seem to endorse a particular
religious viewpoint.

The strategies used to oppose the teaching of evolution in schools
have steadily evolved to try to meet these legal restrictions and have
failed to do so.

To briefly recapitulate this legal history, in the early days of the republic, public schools taught a generic Protestant-based ideology and the King James Bible. But even before Charles Darwin and Alfred Wallace announced the theory of evolution by natural selection in 1858, the idea of separation of church and state had gained ground in the United States and, by the end of the nineteenth century, had largely resulted in the elimination of formal and institutionalized religious instruction and the Bible from schools.

As the theory of evolution by natural selection gained acceptance and became widely taught in public school classrooms in the early days of the twentieth century, those sensitive to its negative implications for religion sought to neutralize what they viewed as an antireligious doctrine.

The first attempts at counteracting the rising influence of evolutionary ideas took the form of state legislatures passing laws banning its teaching, with the 1925 Butler Act in Tennessee being the first. While this act triggered the famous Scopes trial, it was only in 1968, in the case of *Epperson v. Arkansas*, that the U.S. Supreme Court ruled that such attempts were unconstitutional.

Attempts at neutralizing the teaching of evolution then shifted to the second phase, away from outright bans on teaching evolution to efforts to achieve "balanced treatment" (whatever that meant) for both evolution and the Genesis story of creation. But the U.S. Sixth Circuit Court of Appeals ruled the Tennessee law requiring this unconstitutional in the 1975 case of *Daniel v. Waters*.

The third attempted strategy was to call for "balanced treatment" for the teaching of evolution and something called "creation science," the latter being essentially the young-Earth Genesis story carefully shorn of any mention of God or the Bible or any religious language. Such laws were passed in 1981 in both Arkansas and Louisiana. A U.S. district court ruled the Arkansas law unconstitutional in 1982 in *McLean v. Arkansas Board of Education*, and the U.S. Supreme Court ruled the Louisiana law unconstitutional in 1987 in the case of *Edwards v. Aguillard*.

This setback gave rise to the fourth and final attempt, which no longer sought balance but instead tried to undermine the credibility of the theory of evolution and to eliminate methodological naturalism as a working principle for scientific investigations. The theory of intelligent design, created for this purpose, was carefully crafted to try to address all the objections raised by these legal precedents.

Its essential strategy was to allege that certain systems in nature (the bacterial flagellum, the blood-clotting mechanism, and the human immune system being most frequently invoked) were "irreducibly complex"; not only had evolutionary theory failed so far to provide an adequate explanation for how they could have come into being by the gradual mechanism of natural selection, but the theory would *never* be able to explain their existence.

This unsubstantiated assertion allowed intelligent design advocates to make the inference that these systems were deliberately designed and abruptly created; hence, there must be some "designer" at work. The identity of the designer was deliberately kept unspecified and, like Lord Voldemort in the Harry Potter books, was rarely named openly, but there was never any doubt that the intelligent designer referred to was God.

This latest hope for undermining the teaching of evolution in public schools was dashed by the 2005 verdict in *Kitzmiller v. Dover Area School District*, in which a U.S. district court ruled that by appealing to what were effectively supernatural forces, intelligent design was a religious belief and not science and that because the reason for introducing it into the curriculum was to advance a religious agenda, such a policy was unconstitutional.

So the religious forces, having lost the scientific case against evolution (basically because they never had a scientific case to start with, just a religious belief adorned with scientific language), now have pretty much lost the legal case as well. And that is where things stand.

Interestingly, the current legal state of play supports what Clarence Darrow argued back in 1926 in the appeal to the Tennessee

---

Tammy Kitzmiller was the lead plaintiff in the 2005 trial *Kitzmiller v. Dover Area School District*, which resulted in intelligent design's being found to be a religious belief and thus its teaching in public schools a violation of the Establishment Clause. She works as an office manager and is the mother of two daughters, one of whom was in ninth-grade biology at the time the *Dover* policy was implemented, thus one of its targets.

Supreme Court of the *Scopes* verdict. He maintained that opposition to the theory of evolution was not designed to foster neutrality in education but essentially sprang from a religious foundation that was hostile to science. Thus, any attempt to suppress its teaching was an attempt to advance religious views at the expense of science, and this went counter to the purposes of public schools.

Given this legal history, it is not clear what other avenues are available for efforts to resurrect intelligent design creationism or some new variant as a viable legal strategy against Darwin's theory. Attempts seem to have shifted to an almost exclusively public relations effort by the Discovery Institute, the organization that has been behind the intelligent design strategy all along. Its representatives' attempts to push back against the *Dover* disaster is taking many forms, ranging from attacking Judge John E. Jones III's bona fides, making documentaries charging that intelligent design advocates are being persecuted and hounded out of academia, and writing books to take their case to the general public.

It seems as though now that intelligent design advocates have lost in both the courts and the scientific arena, they are reduced to portraying themselves as victims and making pleas for public sympathy to try to convince people that the scientific and legal establishments have somehow conspired to use their muscle to suppress alternatives to the theory of evolution.

Conspicuously missing in all these efforts by the religious opponents of evolution is any actual old-fashioned *science*: experiments done, data collected, hypotheses formulated, causal mechanisms suggested that can be used to make concrete predictions that can be investigated, and the publishing of such work in recognized peer-reviewed scientific journals. In other words, they are not doing the kind of detailed, careful, painstaking work that Darwin carried out and that constitutes the bedrock of science. Grand, sweeping, and speculative ideas can be fun for a while, but if not supported by a solid foundation of evidence and data, they sink and disappear, leaving very little trace.

Herbert Spencer pointed out this curious and fatal weakness of evolution's opponents as long ago as 1891: "Those who cavalierly reject the Theory of Evolution as not being adequately supported by facts, seem to forget that their own theory is supported by no facts at all."[2]

So, who will emerge as the eventual victor in the case of *God v. Darwin*? The jury is, of course, still out, but one can safely predict that while Darwin may or may not win in the end, God definitely will not.

The reason is simple. The history of science since Copernicus clearly demonstrates that while scientific theories can overthrow religious beliefs and have done so numerous times, the reverse simply does not happen.

Religious people have not grasped (or perhaps do not want to grasp) the fact that Darwin's theory will never be replaced by a religious belief structure because religious beliefs cannot overthrow a scientific theory. What overthrows a scientific theory is a *better scientific theory*.

In the final analysis, it is as simple as that.

NOTES

1. Daniel C. Dennett, *Darwin's Dangerous Idea* (New York: Simon & Schuster, 1995).

2. Herbert Spencer, *Essays Scientific, Political & Speculative* (New York: D. Appleton and Company, 1891).

Appendix

Court Cases

(UPPER CASE refers to Supreme Court decisions, **bold** refers to cases involving evolution. The chapters that discuss those cases are in square brackets.)

1. GITLOW v. NEW YORK, 268 U.S. 652 (1925) [chapters 5, 9]
   www.law.cornell.edu/supct/html/historics/USSC_CR_0268_
   0652_ZS.html

   This case extended the due process clause of the Fourteenth Amendment to include the freedom of speech and press protections of the First Amendment to cover actions by state and local governments as well.

2. The State of Tennessee v. John Thomas Scopes [chapters 5, 6, 7]
   Scopes v. State, 152 Tenn. 424, 278 S.W. 57 (Tenn. 1925)

   This is the grandfather of all evolution trials, which set the stage for all the evolution cases that followed. John T. Scopes was found guilty of teaching the theory of evolution in violation of the Butler Act of Tennessee. Scopes's conviction was overturned by the Tennessee Supreme Court on a technicality, even as that court upheld the constitutionality of the law forbidding the teaching of evolution.

3. CANTWELL v. CONNECTICUT, 310 U.S. 296 (1940) [chapter 9]
   www.law.cornell.edu/supct/html/historics/USSC_CR_0310_
   0296_ZS.html

   This case upheld the right of Jehovah's Witnesses to spread their message on a public street without getting prior government approval and in the process extended the reach of the free exercise of religion clause of the First Amendment to cover actions by state and local governments as well by virtue of the due process clause of the Fourteenth Amendment.

4. EVERSON v. BOARD OF EDUCATION OF EWING TP., 330 U.S. 1 (1947) [chapters 8, 9]
   www.law.cornell.edu/supct/html/historics/USSC_CR_0330_0001_ZS.html

The Supreme Court upheld by a 5–4 vote the policy of a local school district in New Jersey to reimburse parents for the cost of bus transportation for their children to attend parochial schools. In the process it asserted that the Establishment Clause of the First Amendment was binding on state and local governments as well by virtue of the due process clause of the Fourteenth Amendment. The case also marked the appearance of Thomas Jefferson's "wall of separation" phrase into constitutional legal opinion.

5. McCOLLUM v. BOARD OF EDUCATION, 333 U.S. 203 (1948) [chapters 8, 9]
   www.law.cornell.edu/supct/html/historics/USSC_CR_0333_0203_ZS.html

This case involved a challenge to the practice of public schools granting "release time" for the teaching of religion in school buildings during the school day to those students and parents who agreed to it. The U.S. Supreme Court by an 8–1 vote ruled the policy unconstitutional. This was the first time that religious instruction in public schools was first explicitly ruled to be unconstitutional under the U.S. Constitution.

6. ZORACH v. CLAUSON, 343 U.S. 306 (1952) [chapter 9]
   www.law.cornell.edu/supct/html/historics/USSC_CR_0343_0306_ZS.html

This was also a release-time case, but since the students left the school buildings for religious instruction, it was ruled constitutional by a narrow margin.

7. ENGEL v. VITALE, 370 U.S. 421 (1962) [chapter 9]
   www.law.cornell.edu/supct/html/historics/USSC_CR_0370_0421_ZS.html

This case involved students beginning each day by saying a prayer composed by the New York Board of Regents. The Supreme Court ruled 6–1 that governmentally composed prayers in public schools were unconstitutional, even if students were not compelled to say them.

8. SCHOOL DISTRICT OF ABINGTON TOWNSHIP, PENNSYLVANIA v. SCHEMPP, 374 U.S. 203 (1963) [chapter 9] www.law.cornell.edu/supct/html/historics/USSC_CR_0374_0203_ZS.html

The U.S. Supreme Court ruled 8–1 that no state law or school board may require that passages from the Bible be read or that the Lord's Prayer be recited in public schools.

9. **EPPERSON v. ARKANSAS, 393 U.S. 97** (1968) [chapters 7, 10, 17, 20] www.law.cornell.edu/supct/html/historics/USSC_CR_0393_0097_ZS.html

The U.S. Supreme Court ruled unanimously that a 1928 Arkansas law forbidding the teaching of evolution was unconstitutional.

10. LEMON v. KURTZMAN, 403 U.S. 602 (1971) [chapters 11, 12, 15] www.law.cornell.edu/supct/html/historics/USSC_CR_0403_0602_ZS.html

The Lemon case arose from two separate cases bundled together that allowed the state to reimburse nonpublic schools for nonreligious instructional purposes. In ruling these two policies unconstitutional by votes of 8–0 and 8–1, the Supreme Court promulgated what is now called the three-pronged "Lemon test" for adjudicating violations of the Establishment Clause. It ruled that such reimbursement policies would result in violations of the entanglement prong of the Lemon test.

11. **Daniel v. Waters, (1975) 515 F.2d 485 (6th Cir. 1975)** [chapters 11, 20] www.talkorigins.org/faqs/daniel-v-waters.html

This case arose from a 1974 Tennessee law requiring "balanced treatment" of the teaching of evolution with the teaching of biblical theories of creation. The U.S. Sixth Court of Appeals ruled that such policies clearly gave preferential treatment to religious beliefs and thus violated the Establishment Clause.

12. **McLean v. Arkansas Board of Education, (1981) 529 F. Supp. 1255 (E.D. Ark. 1982)** [chapters 12, 17, 19, 20]
    http://fp.bio.utk.edu/evo-eco/resources-this_semester/McLean%20v_%20Arkansas%20Board%20of%20Education.htm

    This case arose out of a 1981 Arkansas law requiring "balanced treatment" of "creation science" and "evolution science." The district court ruled that it failed all three prongs of the Lemon test for the Establishment Clause.

13. LYNCH v. DONNELLY, 465 U.S. 668 (1984) [chapters 15, 17]
    www.law.cornell.edu/supct/html/historics/USSC_CR_0465_0668_ZS.html

    This case involved the display of a nativity scene by a municipality and introduced the endorsement test for constitutionality under the Establishment Clause, which said that the government cannot take any action that could be viewed as either endorsement or disapproval of religion.

14. **EDWARDS v. AGUILLARD, 482 U.S. 578 (1987)** [chapters 11, 17, 20]
    www.law.cornell.edu/supct/html/historics/USSC_CR_0482_0578_ZO.html

    This case was another "balanced treatment" for "creation science" and "evolution science." The U.S. Supreme Court ruled 7–2 that it failed to meet all three prongs of the Lemon test and that creation science was a religious belief since it invoked a supernatural agency.

15. COUNTY OF ALLEGHENY V. AMERICAN CIVIL LIBERTIES UNION, GREATER PITTSBURGH CHAPTER, 492 U.S. 573 (1989) [chapter 15]
    www.law.cornell.edu/supct/html/historics/USSC_CR_0492_0573_ZS.html

    This was a case challenging the display of a crèche and menorah in a county courthouse at Christmas. The U.S. Supreme Court ruled 5–4 that the crèche was unconstitutional and that the Constitution requires the government to be secular. It denied that prohibiting government from celebrating Christmas as a religious holiday could be interpreted as favoring non-Christians over Christians.

16. **Webster v. New Lenox School District, 917 F. 2d 1004** (1990) [Chapter 12]

The U.S. Seventh Court of Appeals upheld a District Court ruling that a teacher's free speech rights are not violated by a school district preventing him from teaching creation science.

17. **Peloza v. Capistrano Unified School District 37 F.3d 517 (1994)** [Chapter 12]

The U.S. Ninth Court of Appeals upheld a District Court ruling rejecting the argument that "evolutionism" is a religion and that thus requiring teachers to teach it violated the teacher's rights under the Free Speech and Establishment Clauses of the First Amendment and the Due Process and Equal Protection clauses of the Fourteenth Amendment.

18. SANTA FE INDEPENDENT SCHOOL DISTRICT v. DOE, 530 U.S. 290 (2000) [chapter 15] www.law.cornell.edu/supct/html/historics/USSC_CR_0530_0290_ZS.html

In a 6–3 ruling, the U.S. Supreme Court said that a school district's practice of having one student deliver a prayer over the public address system before each home varsity football game was unconstitutional.

19. ELK GROVE UNIFIED SCHOOL DIST. v. NEWDOW, (02-1624) 542 U.S. 1 (2004) [chapters 15, 17] www.law.cornell.edu/supct/html/02-1624.ZS.html

The Supreme Court overturned by an 8–0 vote a lower court ruling that having students in schools say "under God" in the Pledge of Allegiance was unconstitutional. Five justices did so on procedural grounds, and only three justices went into the merits of the case, saying that including the phrase was constitutional. This case said that the issue of whether an endorsement of a particular religious view had occurred had to be made from the perspective of an informed, reasonable observer who embodies a community ideal of social and rational judgment and who "does not evaluate a practice in isolation from its origins and context. Instead, the reasonable observer must be deemed aware of the history of the conduct in question, and must understand its place in our Nation's cultural landscape."

20. **Selman v. Cobb County School District, (2005) 390 F. Supp 2d** [chapter 15] www.talkorigins.org/faqs/cobb/selman-v-cobb.html

This case involved a challenge to a school board's policy of inserting a sticker into biology textbooks undermining the credibility of the theory of evolution. The district court ruled that the sticker policy passed the purpose prong of the Lemon test but failed the effect prong and the endorsement test and was thus unconstitutional. The U.S. Court of Appeals vacated the decision due to the incompleteness of the record on appeal and referred the case back to the lower court. The school district settled the case by agreeing to remove the stickers.

21. **Kitzmiller et al. v. Dover Area School District et al., (2005) 400 F. Supp. 2d 707 (M.D. Pa.)** [chapters 16, 17, 18, 19, 20]
www.pamd.uscourts.gov/kitzmiller/kitzmiller_342.pdf

This case arose from a school board's adopting a policy requiring students in a biology class to have a statement read to them saying that evolution was only a theory, not a fact, and referring students to a book describing the alternate theory of intelligent design. The district court ruled that this policy failed the purpose and effect prongs of the Lemon test, as well as the endorsement test, and that intelligent design was effectively a religious belief since it invoked a supernatural agency.

22. **MCCREARY COUNTY, KENTUCKY, ET AL., v. AMERICAN CIVIL LIBERTIES UNION OF KENTUCKY ET AL., (2005) 545 U.S. 844** [chapter 19]
www.law.cornell.edu/supct/html/03-1693.ZC.html

In this case, the Supreme Court ruled 5–4 that displaying the Ten Commandments in courthouses violated the Establishment Clause.

Bibliography

Behe, Michael. *Darwin's Black Box*. New York: Free Press, 1996.

———. *The Edge of Evolution: The Search for the Limits to Darwinism*. New York: Free Press, 2007.

Bowler, Peter J. *The Eclipse of Darwinism*. Baltimore: Johns Hopkins University Press, 1983.

Darwin, Charles. *On the Origin of Species*. London: John Murray, 1859.

Dawkins, Richard. *The God Delusion*. Boston: Houghton Mifflin, 2006.

Dennett, Daniel C. *Darwin's Dangerous Idea*. New York: Simon & Schuster, 1995.

Desmond, Adrian, and James Moore. *Darwin: The Life of a Tortured Evolutionist*. New York: W. W. Norton & Company, 1991.

DeWolf, David K., John G. West, Casey Luskin, and Jonathan Witt. *Traipsing into Evolution*. Seattle, WA: Discovery Institute, 2006.

Forrest, Barbara, and Paul R. Gross. *Creationism's Trojan Horse: The Wedge of Intelligent Design*. Oxford: Oxford University Press, 2004.

Gish, Duane. *Evolution: The Fossils Say No!* Green Forest, AZ: Master Books, 1978.

Hamburger, Philip. *Separation of Church and State*. Cambridge, MA: Harvard University Press, 2002.

Hamilton, Marci A. *God v. the Gavel: Religion and the Rule of Law*. New York: Cambridge University Press, 2005.

Harris, Sam. *Letter to a Christian Nation*. New York: Knopf, 2006.

———. *The End of Faith*. New York: W. W. Norton & Company, 2004.

Johnson, Phillip. *Darwin on Trial*. Washington, DC: Regnery, 1991.

Kramnick, Isaac, and R. Laurence Moore. *The Godless Constitution: The Case Against Religious Correctness*. New York: W. W. Norton & Company, 1996.

Larson, Edward J. *Summer for the Gods*. Cambridge, MA: Harvard University Press, 1997.

Levy, Leonard W. *The Establishment Clause: Religion and the First Amendment.* Chapel Hill: The University of North Carolina, 1994

Miller, Kenneth R. *Finding Darwin's God.* New York: HarperCollins, 1999.

Moran, Jeffrey P. *The Scopes Trial: A Brief History with Documents.* Boston: Bedford/St. Martins, 2002.

Morris, Simon Conway. *The Crucible of Creation.* Oxford: Oxford University Press, 1998.

Numbers, Ronald. *The Creationists.* New York: Random House, 1992.

Provine, William B. *The Origins of Theoretical Population Genetics.* Chicago: University of Chicago Press, 2001.

Ruse, Michael, ed. *But Is It Science?* Amherst, NY: Prometheus Books, 1996.

Shanks, Niall. *God, the Devil, and Darwin.* Oxford: Oxford University Press, 2004.

Simpson, G. G. *Tempo and Mode in Evolution.* New York: Columbia University Press, 1944.

Singham, Mano. *Quest for Truth: Scientific Progress and Religious Beliefs.* Bloomington, IN: Phi Delta Kappan Educational Foundation, 2000.

Stenger, Victor. *God: The Failed Hypothesis.* Amherst, NY: Prometheus Books, 2007.

Wells, Jonathan. *Icons of Evolution.* Washington, DC: Regnery, 2000.

Whitcomb, John, and Henry M. Morris. *The Genesis Flood.* Phillipsburg, NJ: P&R Publishing, 1961.

Index

theistic evolution, 16–18
Thomas, Clarence, 118
Thomas More Law Center (TMLC), 124, 126–29, 132
Thompson, Richard, 128–29

Unification Church, 102–3
U.S. Supreme Court, vii, viii, 1–2, 32–33, 53–55, 57, 67–74, 79–80, 84, 87–90, 97, 99, 113, 116–18, 125, 131, 133–34, 138, 143, 155, 159–64

Virginia, 59–60, 65

Walcott, Charles Doolittle, 110

wall of separation, 62, 65, 70–71, 104, 121, 154, 160
Wallace, Alfred Russell, 12, 147, 155
Webster v. New Lenox, 99–100, 162
Wedge strategy, 104–5, 107, 123, 125, 129, 135, 140
Wells, H. G., 28
Wells, Jonathan, 101–4
West, John, 128–29, 152
Whitcomb, John, 78, 85
Witt, Jonathan, 152
Wright, Sewall, 11

Zoonomia, 9
Zorach v. Clauson, 72, 75, 160

About the Author

Mano Singham is director of UCITE (University Center for Innovation in Teaching and Education) and adjunct associate professor of physics at Case Western Reserve University, Cleveland, Ohio. He received his B.Sc. (First Class Honors in physics) from the University of Colombo, Sri Lanka, and his M.S. and Ph.D. degrees from the University of Pittsburgh.

After starting out in theoretical medium energy physics, his more recent research interests have been in the fields of education, theories of knowledge, and the history and philosophy of science. He is a Fellow of the American Physical Society and in 2001 won Case Western Reserve University's Carl F. Wittke award for distinguished undergraduate teaching. He has received numerous other awards for teaching and service to education.

He is the author of *Quest for Truth: Scientific Progress and Religious Beliefs* (2000) and *The Achievement Gap in US Education: Canaries in the Mine* (2005).